Information Literacy: Search Strategies, Tools, & Resources for High School Students

Zorana Ercegovac

Linworth Publishing
Worthington, Ohio

Library of Congress Cataloging-in-Publication Data

Ercegovac, Zorana, 1947-
  Information literacy : search strategies, tools & resources for high school students /
Zorana Ercegovac.
    p. cm. -- (Professional growth series)
  Includes bibliographical references and index.
  ISBN 1-58683-021-X (perfectbound)
    1. Library orientation for high school students--United States. 2. Information
retrieval--Study and teaching (Secondary)--United States. 3. Information literacy--Study
and teaching (Secondary)--United States. I. Title. II. Series.

Z711.2.E7 2001
027.62'6--dc21

                                                                            2001029305

Published by Linworth Publishing, Inc.
480 East Wilson Bridge Road, Suite L
Worthington, Ohio 43085

Series Information:
From The Professional Growth Series

ISBN 1-58683-021-X

5 4 3 2 1

Table of Contents

■ **About the Author** **169**

■ **Index** **171**

List of Figures and Tables

List of Exercises

Acknowledgments

The greatest contribution to this work has come from my daughter Una. She contributed in important ways from the beginning of this project to its final product. Una read numerous versions of the entire manuscript many times over the past several years, and contributed to this work as an editor, consultant, and a supporter. My husband Miloš D. Ercegovac contributed to all technical, many conceptual, and affective aspects of the work. Special thanks go to my children Una and Vuk who helped in many different ways throughout all phases of this effort.

I wish to thank Thomas Gilder, Head of Windward School for his support and encouragement. The following teachers contributed in important ways in improving this book: Eric Mandel of the History Department; Paul Slocombe of the Science Department; and Paula Hirsch of the Foreign Language Department. Special thanks go to Mark Simpson, the Director of Upper School and Shirley Windward, the co-founder of Windward School.

I am grateful to Betty Morris, an acquisition editor with Linworth Publishing, who encouraged me to publish this book. Appreciation must go to the reviewers, who generously donated their time in critiquing this manuscript.

I also wish to thank UCLA's Department of Information Studies for giving me the opportunity to teach a 4-unit undergraduate information literacy course (1991–1998). I am indebted to many graduate library students for constructive comments. Further appreciation is extended to college and public instructional librarians and, in particular, teachers in the Los Angeles area. Currently, I am the Director of Library and Information Studies and the School Archivist at Windward. I continue to lead the InfoEN Associates consulting firm in all aspects of curriculum-embedded information literacy.

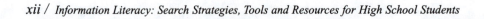

Preface

Goal and audience

This book has been designed as a practical guide to information literacy programs for high schools. It will be especially useful to media specialists, instructional librarians, and teachers as a guide to teaching information literacy skills for grades 9-12. The book is written in a way that can easily be used by college-bound high school students, and freshmen in community colleges and universities. In addition, schools of library and information studies may want to use this book, with some modifications, in two different ways: first, as an introductory text to orient first-year library students to the basics of information access and basic resources; and second, as a primer in bibliographic instruction courses, also known as user education and library instruction.

Objectives

The overall objective of this book is to help all students become competent learners. By the end of this information literacy program (ILP), students will learn how to:

- **Plan their research.** The Big Picture. To this end, students will start off by reading Chapter 1. It will introduce the students to basic library skills and competencies. It will also help define information needs and spaces. Students as PLANNERS.
- **Organize their preparation for searching.** Chapter 2, Finding Search Words, and Chapter 3, Search Strategies, will become students' main guides for brainstorming. Students as PROBLEM SOLVERS.
- **Find a variety of resources on their selected topic.** Chapters 4 through 8 will introduce the student to multiple information resources beyond the school walls. Students as SEARCHERS and EVALUATORS.
- **Think critically about resources and give credit to the works used in their own writings.** Chapter 9 will show how to utilize the best resources for a report. The Chapter focuses on summarizing and making terrific bibliographies. Students as SCHOLARS.

Here are several scenarios that illustrate uses of this book:

- **Scenario 1:** A high school history teacher collaborates with a media specialist to introduce students in critical thinking skills of Web resources for history presentations and written papers. Students read Chapter 7 that deals with Internet searching and other issues. The teacher introduces the importance of giving credit related to Web documents (Chapter 9).

Teacher supplements Chapters 7 and 9 with some of the Appendices (I–J, B) and Think Guide for Chapter 7 (evaluation of Web sources). Alternatively, instructors may modify Think Guides and hand out their customized versions to students.

■ **Scenario 2:** In a high school with a single professional media specialist, teachers ask students to use resources for their reports. A busy librarian offers on-demand assistance and needs to consult our book for illustrations, collaborative projects, and fruitful ideas that can be easily applied or modified. This book provides plenty of exercises, list of sources, ideas in individual chapters as well as in eleven Appendices, four Think Guides, and an Index.

■ **Scenario 3:** Media specialists use the book as a guide to teaching information literacy skills for grades 9-12. Some of the Think Guides are used in their current form or with minor modifications for in-class exercises (see list of exercises) and examples (see list of Figures and Tables). Teachers may want to use the text as a script for their own teaching, as a model for further refinement and customization, and as a recommended text to, say, all high school, college-bound students. The word "you" in this book (Chapters 1-9) refers to the high school student who is learning information literacy skills within his or her subject matter, such as social studies, the arts, and the sciences. Whichever modality this books will be used in, I hope that I have provided sufficient amount of material, through its main chapters, the Annotated Bibliography, Think Guides, Appendices, and the Web resources, that you will find this book a useful resource in your busy and important work.

Organization

The book is divided into nine chapters. The first three chapters are general and apply to searching, regardless of the format or medium (Chapter 1). We search by means of selecting search words. What are search words, where to find them, and how to use them? Answers to these questions are in Chapter 2. Whether you search CD-ROM databases, Web-based magazine and newspaper articles, or online library catalogs, you need to know certain basic skills and search techniques that apply to all sources (Chapter 3). Chapter 9 applies to another set of research skills. It shows how to cite and summarize writings that students read and choose to include in their own writings.

Chapters 4 through 8 include various resources in the order these sources are typically used in the process of library research. Chapter 4, Fact Finding: words, concepts, events, places, covers dictionaries, encyclopedias, factbooks, as well as maps, atlases, and gazetteers. Chapter 5, Fact Finding: people, reviews, criticism, covers related resources regardless of their medium. Chapter 6 is on online library catalogs: what they are, which questions are appropriate to using library catalogs, and how to use them. Chapter 7 is on Internet resources. Chapter 8 is on accessing magazine and newspaper articles. The entire book can be covered during a single term; this author, as you can see in the Schedule <http://www.windwardlibrary.net>, has covered most of this book in a five-week period.

Special features of this book include four Think Guides and eleven Appendices that supplement and enhance individual Chapters as follows:

Chapter	Appendices	Think Guides (TG)
1 Introduction to Basic Research Skills	C Lesson plan collaboration D IL baseline pre-test E Scoring rubrics F Post-test	TG for Chapter 1: Topic narrowing
2 Finding Search Words	A Dewey Decimal Classification (DDC)	TG for Chapter 2: Finding Search Words
3 Search Strategies		TG for Chapter 3: Search Strategies can be used in Chapters 7 and 8.
4 Fact Finding: words, concepts, events, places	See Appendix K: Sources	
5 Fact Finding: people, reviews, criticism	See Appendix K: Sources	
6 Finding books, maps, reference sources		TG for Chapter 2: Finding Search Words; TG for Chapter 3: Search Strategies
7 Searching & Evaluating Internet Sources	B Acceptable Use Agreement G Metacognition (can be used throughout the book)	TG for Chapter 3: Search Strategies; TG for Chapter 4: Evaluation of Web Sources
8 Finding Magazine & Newspaper Articles	H Online Database	TG for Chapter 3: Search Strategies
9 Citing in Style and Summarizing	I Citing in Style J Summarizing sources	
Annotated Bibliography		
Index		

Table P1: Organization of this book

The information literacy program (ILP or Program) that is described in this book is comprehensive because it contains references to a variety of sources and digital collections, introduces effective search strategies and tools for the use of these sources, and covers critical evaluation of these sources. Within this one-stop literacy mall, the Program also offers about 40 exercises and a glossary of introduced terms and concepts. It features more than 100 selected Internet addresses of numerous sources that are available on the Web.

The book is tested in classroom and computer lab settings with students who had little or no information literacy skills. Collaborative work with teachers in history, science, foreign languages, and the arts, has helped this work evolve into a curriculum-integrated and project-supported program. For weekly coverage of the information literacy program, see its schedule at <http://www.windwardlibrary.net>.

The book is flexible: the content is divided into a series of interrelated yet independent chapters. This means that you do not have to start with Chapter 1 and proceed sequentially to Chapter 2, and end with Chapter 9. However, starting off with Chapter 1, which covers some basic library and research skills, may help as your first selection.

Reasons why a school librarian should use this book:

This book is based in empirical research, and has been validated in a real classroom environment with students. Teachers' feedback has been incorporated as well as the School Reform (curriculum standards; alignment between and among various instructional materials including lessons, handouts, texts, exercises, tests and so forth; scoring rubrics). In addition, check out our Web library home page for details and the schedule of our weekly information literacy scope and coverage <http://www.windwardlibrary.net/>.

The author of this book has had the classroom experience both in high school curriculum as well as in the college instruction. She has seen first hand what students need to know before they come to college. **If you want your students to graduate with information literacy skills, this book is for you.**

The book lists resources (in Appendix K) and describes more than 100 Web sources throughout the book. These will be maintained and kept current via this author's home page<http://www.lainet.com/infoen/>. Annotated Bibliography identifies and summarizes more than 35 major pieces covering various aspects of the information literacy literature.

This book justifies Information Literacy programs to management. No one wants to be behind; schools want to produce excellent graduates, to see them succeed in colleges of their choice. This book will assist you in this regard.

The book translates research from information seeking behavior, information retrieval, and educational psychology into a practical information literacy program for high school teachers, media specialists, students, and parents. The book will ensure that our high school graduates, wherever they go and whatever they pursue, will be well prepared, informed, and self-motivated for the life-long learning journey ahead. The author instructs media specialists and teachers at professional conferences such as California School Library Association (CSLA) on this and related topics. Most recently, at CSLA 2000 in Santa Clara, she presented a workshop titled: Curriculum-Embedded Information Literacy: From Standards to Assessments, and another, What Every College-Bound High School Graduate Should Know: Library Survival Skills. The author of this book has been invited to present Information Literacy position papers at prestigious invitational workshops, including the National Academy of Sciences (for details see <http://www.cs.ucla.edu/Leap/zer>.

CONCEPTUAL FRAMEWORK. This section is of particular importance to media specialists.

The conceptual framework for this work draws on (a) learning theories; (b) research on information seeking of children and young adults; and (c) information literacy within school reform. In addition, the author has been teaching and researching various aspects of information literacy since 1990. For the selected reading list on information literacy models, learning and assessment reports, as well as other relevant texts, readers are referred to the Annotated Bibliography in this book.

LEARNING THEORY. The information literacy approach taken in this book considers the five components of learning: content understanding, problem solving, metacognition, collaboration, and communication. For details, see CRESST reports, body of work produced by Kuhlthau, and separately by Pitts in Annotated Bibliography in back of this book.

This book includes four "think guides" and eleven appendices. Think guides and appendices are designed to highlight each of the five learning components. Each think guide contains two parts: the first part gives a worked out example followed by a form that may be adapted and distributed to students.

Think Guides in support of problem solving include Think Guide for Chapter 1 with topic narrowing examples; Think Guide for Chapter 2 on search words; Think Guide for Chapter 3 on search strategy techniques; and Think Guide for Chapter 7 on evaluation of Web documents. The material on how to evaluate Web sources for their quality may be used in collaborative settings in which students work in small teams to find information, debate on the usefulness of their sources, and present to the class. Examples for collaborative projects are also provided in Appendix C. Each example for collaborative projects prompts the teacher and the media specialist to think about the overall organizational structure of the assigned projects (instructional frameworks, scoring rubrics, objectives of the project, problem-solving activities for the students to work in small teams, and citation templates). We also include separate appendices on assessment techniques, including one on pre-testing and another on scoring indicators. Appendix D includes an example of a pre-test;

Appendix E shows scoring rubrics for information literacy (IL) skills; and Appendix F offers an example for a post-test. There are two appendices with examples for citing various formats and summarizing information sources (see Appendices I and J). Finally, there is an Appendix G on metacognition to help teachers and library media specialists phrase their own questions in order to find students' level of awareness and perception of their self-monitoring, planning, and organizational skills.

In addition to the four think guides and seven appendices that support learning components, there are appendices that are of general interest. Appendix A gives subdivisions of Dewey Decimal Classification main classes; this one can be used throughout the book to remind the students of the main classification scheme in their own libraries. Appendix B may be useful to teachers and media specialists as a guide to thinking about how to write their own Acceptable Use Agreement. It contains an example of an Acceptable Use Agreement that Windward School uses. Appendix H includes a checklist for evaluating online reference services, such as ProQuest, NewsBank, and SirS. It also summarizes these three services and gives contacts and Internet addresses. Each appendix and think guide is linked, whenever possible, to individual chapters in this book. Finally Appendix K lists sources that are mentioned throughout this book.

Table P2 on the next page illustrates how each of these five components of higher level thinking is linked to information literacy skills, and specifically to chapters in this book.

INFORMATION SEEKING RESEARCH APPLIED. Information problem solving and a detailed analysis of cognitive strategies within student's information search process (ISP) have been studied by Kuhlthau (1993; 1997; 1999a; 1999b). Information seeking, according to Kuhlthau, incorporates the experience of interactive thoughts, actions, and feeling in the process of construction. Thoughts relate to the cognitive domain, such as problem solving; actions relate to the sensori-motor domain such as scrolling and navigating through the Web; and feelings relate to the affective domain, such as uncertainty, clarity, interests, likes, dislikes, motivation, and so forth. Other information seeking and information literacy models (e.g., Bates; Eisenberg & Berkowitz; Pitts) are in the Annotated Bibliography of this book.

INFORMATION LITERACY WITHIN SCHOOL REFORM. Some of the above findings are applied in "A position paper on information problem solving" prepared and endorsed by the American Association of School Librarians <http://www.ala.org/aasl/positions/PS_infolit.html>. The position calls for the partnership between teachers and media specialists in order to collaboratively create integrated and resource-based learning experiences. The phrase "resource-based" learning refers to the ability to create knowledge based on the evidence from multiple resources; students learn to access,

Learning Components	Links to Information Literacy Skills
Content understanding	Students learn to see the Big Picture and consider multiple sources across all formats and media; they learn to ask a question and shape their project focus; to differentiate access locators, and to learn characteristics of information sources. Students as PLANNERS (Chapters 1, 4-8, Think Guides for Chapters 1-3, 7 + Appendices)
Problem solving	Students learn to organize their "think pads": plan their search strategies, and find search terms (Chapters 1-3, + Think Guides for Chapters 1-3, 7). Students as PROBLEM SOLVERS.
Collaboration	Students work in small teams to brainstorm, evaluate, present, and peer-teach. Teachers and media specialists collaborate together on IL units. Students as TEAMWORKERS (throughout the book, especially Appendix C).
Metacognition (self-regulation)	Students monitor their progress and timing, improve their strategies, correct errors. (See Appendix G)
Communication	Students communicate their findings via projects, presentations, and annotated bibliographies (Chapter 9 + Appendices I-J). Students as SCHOLARS.

Table P2: CRESST Model of learning linked to IL skills, Chapters, Think Guides, Appendices

locate, interpret, analyze, and apply evidence in order to achieve specific goals. A goal might be to prepare a travel brochure of a particular geographic and cultural region; to take opposing views on a particular historical issue and link it to a current event or phenomenon; or to create a visual of a historical or scientific phenomenon, or a landmark architecture, three dimensional diorama, PowerPoint presentation, or a Web document. Finally, the position paper embraces the restructuring of our schools. This component has not been well incorporated in many existing information literacy models and programs. More work is needed to link higher level cognitive demands with curricular frameworks and assessment instruments. Finally, we do not have as yet well-defined alignment between and among multiple components of the educational environment, such as standards, assessments, texts, resources, homeworks and quizzes, lecture notes, lab notes, and class plans.

In order to help you in assisting your students to become efficient information users and life-long learners, we have developed *Information Literacy: Search Strategies, Tools & Resources for High School Students*, a comprehensive, class-tested, curriculum-integrated, flexible, and project-based information literacy resource. The book takes a student-centered perspective rather than a technological perspective. It focuses on the intellectual aspects of locating, interpreting, evaluating, and communicating information sources, rather than on the technical aspects of these activities.

Introduction to Basic Research Skills

In this chapter, you will learn how:
1. To think about finding information of interest that will become useful in your projects
   - understand basic ways information is organized
   - learn to use a variety of information sources
   - identify characteristics of information sources
2. To ask a good question
   - recognize and express information needs
   - focus a term-paper on the topic of your choice
3. To use library language effectively

Chapter 1 introduces the different ways information is organized and searched. It discusses important characteristics of information sources that experts find useful in locating information. This chapter shows how to express information need and map it into a good question. It is necessary to begin by defining the essential terms and concepts (e.g., access, locate, ask, and meanings of retrieval systems such as library catalogs) that will help you become an educated information user.

To *access* means to retrieve a record representing a physical document. For example, when we search library catalogs, we see many different types of records. These records, despite their differences, typically include the author's name, title of an item, and subject headings; the physical description of an item and publication information may also be given. Through these data elements, records describe physical documents such as books. To *locate* means to retrieve a document, either physically or electronically; the document may be a book, a map, a photograph, or a computer file.

In the example of Franklin of Philadelphia, (below), the author is *Esmond Wright*; the title is *Franklin of Philadelphia*. Subject headings are: *Franklin, Benjamin, 1706–1790*; *Statesmen—United States—Biography*. This means that we can look this book up in the library catalog by the author's name (search under Esmond Wright in either order), title words (use significant title words, Franklin Philadelphia; ignore the preposition "of"), and subject headings (any combination of the words in the two subject headings).

Notice that the words in publication and description fields are not searchable (see Figure 1.1). However, we can browse library shelves in the 973.3092 area (according to the Dewey Decimal Classification, which you will learn in Chapter 2) for biographies of persons who lived in Colonial America. You may find biographies of many prominent early Americans including Adams, Franklin, Hamilton, Jefferson, Marshall, Paine, Revere, and many other famous names all grouped together in the same general area in your library.

Author:　　Wright, Esmond.

Title:　　Franklin of Philadelphia.

Publication: Cambridge, Mass. : Belknap Press of Harvard University Press, 1986.

Physical description:　　xvii, 404 p., [18] p. of plates : ill.; 25cm.

Notes:　　Includes bibliographical references and index.

Subject headings:　　Franklin, Benjamin, 1706-1790.
　　　　　　　　　　　　Statesmen—United States—Biography.

Call number: 973.3 WRI

Figure 1.1: Cataloging entry for Wright's Franklin of Philadelphia book

To access and locate writings by and about Benjamin Franklin, use any of the following retrieval systems, preferably in the following order:

■ **Printed reference sources** include the multi-volume *World Book Encyclopedia*. If you are looking for an article on Franklin, make sure your volume includes letter F on its spine (F for Franklin). The entire Encyclopedia is arranged alphabetically, that is, articles on topics, ideas, places, events, and people are all arranged alphabetically, from A to Z. The last volume contains an index that shows articles on Franklin throughout the multi-volume set. To learn more about encyclopedias, go to Chapter 4.

- **Library catalogs** will show which books are locally available in your own library by and about Benjamin Franklin. As a result of your library search, benjamin franklin, you will see a list of short titles displayed on a computer screen for books that match your search. In order to locate some of these documents, select desired titles one at a time; each selected title will display a detailed cataloging record for the corresponding book including the author's name, full title, publication date, physical description and call number. It is important to write down call numbers for all books that you wish to read and/or borrow from your library. Chapter 6 will give more details on how to find books by means of using library catalogs.

- **Archives** typically include primary documents such as personal letters and correspondence, diaries, costumes of a certain period, and other cultural objects that were a part of a person or an organization. An example is Franklin's Archive in Philadelphia, which is available on the Web; it will take you through a virtual multimedia gallery of his scientific experiments in electricity and other achievements in politics, philosophy, printing, and music writing; you will see his portraits and manuscripts at: <http://sln.fi.edu/franklin/rotten.html>. You will discover many more Web resources in Chapter 7. You will also learn how to identify and select good sites—not everything on the Web is of equally high quality.

- **Remote library catalogs** will show records representing writings by and about Benjamin Franklin that are located remotely—away from your school library. If you searched University of California's online library catalog <http://www.cdlib.org/>, you will see records that describe documents about Franklin's views on the education of youth in Pennsylvania, and his essays on government, ethics, and economy. These documents may be stored in different University of California campus libraries. In order to locate some of these documents, you would have to visit the individual libraries that own writings related to Benjamin Franklin.

- **Online magazine and newspaper databases**, also known as periodical indexes, such as *ProQuest*, *NewsBank*, or *SirS* will give access to magazine and newspaper articles. Some titles might be available in your school library. Others can be obtained from other school libraries through inter-library loan or via the e-mail. Chapter 8 goes into more detail about how to look up magazine articles.

These five types of retrieval systems are organized and searched differently. We suggest that you start your search with encyclopedias and the school library catalog. It will point to books and other reference sources that are closest to you.

To *ask a good question* means to express an information need as broad or as specific as the need may be. For example, if you wanted to find books on the origins or causes of the American Revolution, your question should not be at the level of U.S. politics and government in general or about the state of Massachusetts in particular.

Psychologists, physicians, engineers, and other professionals, have each developed their own language to communicate their ideas effectively. You will be a better researcher if you are comfortable with terms such as reference sources and the differences among a variety of sources, classification schemes, and library catalogs; other library-related activities include inter-library loan, and borrowing policies. These concepts, along with those pertaining to evaluating, citing, and summarizing (see Chapters 4, 7 and 9), finding good search terms (see Chapter 2), and constructing search strategies (see Chapter 3) are the foundation of knowing how to access, locate, interpret, and evaluate sources. Especially important are Think Guides, located at the end of corresponding chapters, and Appendices in the back of this book.

Location of informal information sources (unpublished material)

It is useful to consider the communication process in the broader context of locating information (see Figure 1.2). In such a setting, the simplest communication model, referred to as Model 1, operates under the general assumption that there is a sender who initiates a message (CREATOR), and a receiver of that message (USER).

Model 1 assumes that messages exchanged between the creator and the user are of short duration, informal in nature, and interactive regardless of the place and their content. Messages are exchanged electronically via e-mail, face-to-face, by phone, and fax. Students and teachers transfer their files remotely, and participate in debates from virtual classrooms. In each of these settings people can modify their behavior and messages instantly to account for specific age groups, language skills, literacy levels, and cultural differences. There is no imposed system of organization on the informal information sources other than their inner file organization.

CREATOR ⟶ USER

Informal Communication
- short messages
- interaction between creator and user

Examples:
- face-to-face debate
- phone/fax messages
- electronic mail (e-mail)
- public speaking

Figure 1.2: Communication — Model 1

Location of formal information sources (published material)

Figure 1.3 represents a more complex level of communication between the creator and the user. As messages become longer, they get published in a variety of formats, such as books, magazine articles, music albums, and software programs. This recorded knowledge is stored in bookstores and libraries; it is arranged in various ways. Since the famed Alexandria library before the first century A.D., people have worked hard to organize recorded knowledge for different purposes. On one side of the spectrum is the example of a personal library where documents may be organized by size, by most recently acquired material, and by quality—a stack of good books. A bookstore organizes its publications by means of classifying them by fiction, nonfiction, best sellers, biographies, cookbooks, and travel; other clearinghouses may use multiple copies of titles: one copy under fiction, another under author's name, yet another as a best seller, and so on. While these different schemes may suffice in small collections, they are often inadequate for large collections. Thus, there is an additional layer of organization—the catalog, as illustrated in Model 3.

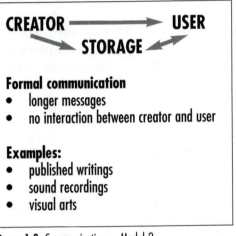

Figure 1.3: Communication—Model 2

Location of information via "filters": Finding a needle in a haystack

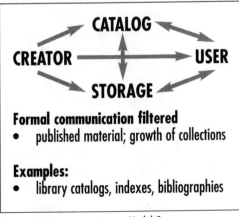

Figure 1.4: Communication—Model 3

Model 3 has an additional layer between the creator and the user (see Figure 1.4). While readers can go directly to a library or bookstore and browse its material, it may be faster and more efficient to first search a catalog—an example of a filter between documents and users. Other filtering mechanisms include bibliographies, such as Books in Print, or publications on the Internet: http://www.amazon.com/; and magazine online databases, also known as periodical indexes (e.g., *ProQuest* <http://proquest.umi.com>, *NewsBank*, or *SirS*). Catalogs are designed to rapidly lead you to desired items in a collection. This model assumes that there is a fairly large collection of material and that the user is familiar with library organization. Library catalogs have added unique features to the library organization in the following two ways:

1. A catalog has an additional layer between the author or creator and the user; it allows library items to be arranged according to a classification scheme, not sequentially, in the order in which items arrive to the library, or according to broad topics (e.g., Yahoo!'s top level categories such as arts and humanities, news and media, recreation and sports, society and culture, science).

2. Each library item is identified, described, classified, and given a call number that uniquely represents that item. Call numbers are independent of a specific shelf location; they are only linked to the item.

How people look up information: From hunter-gatherer to sophisticated user

The most common way of looking up information is random, exploratory and not planned out in advance (see Figure 1.5). Therefore, you are "hunting and gathering" bits of information as you go along.

The setting may be a bookstore, personal files, or your library. This informal information seeking style may lead to surprising discoveries. The process of exploration, while time consuming, is an important learning experience.

The next stage of information seeking is more directed than the one of the Hunter/Gatherer. Scanning presumes a certain organizational structure in place (see Figure 1.6).

USER ⟶ CREATOR

Model 1: Hunter-Gatherer
- picking up bits of information from areas which are most likely to give desired results

Examples:
- browsing and exploring through bookstores, libraries, and personal files

Figure 1.5: Seeking behavior — Model 1

USER ⟶ CREATOR
TITLES

Model 2: Early thinker
- a more directed and systematic search to determine the utility of relevant titles

Examples:
- scanning titles of the most promising publishers and/or authors
- skimming over content pages of books and magazines

Figure 1.6: Seeking behavior — Model 2

Search, for example, for titles published by W. W. Norton on the Colonial period, 1600–1775. Chances are that there will be only a few titles on this topic.

If you are a fairly sophisticated searcher, you will use retrieval filters, including library catalogs and other indexes, in order to locate desired materials on your topic.

The following section will show a roadmap to locating sources.

Search strategy roadmap

The strategy assumes that the student is an *inexperienced* library searcher. Let's assume that the student is a tourist in a town never visited before.

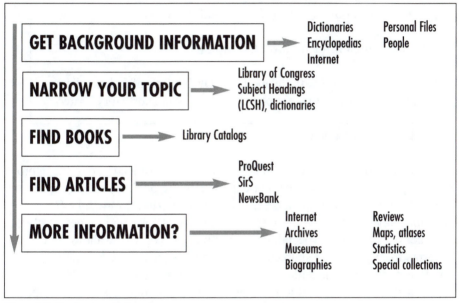

Figure 1.7: Roadmap to sources

Chances are that a map of that town would help demystify road patterns and streets, give some orientation, point to interesting places, and give an overall sense of the town. To use this analogy in a library setting, we show a roadmap to information sources (see Figure 1.7). Start off by using encyclopedias to get the big picture. Examples are *World Book Encyclopedia* and *Encyclopedia Britannica* <http://www.eb.com/> (see Chapter 4). Before you use the library catalog, look up search words in the big red books (LCSH) that your librarian will explain (see Chapter 2). Use these words to search the library catalog and find books in your school library (Chapters 3, 6). To access magazine and newspaper articles, search magazine databases such as *ProQuest* (Chapter 8). Internet and biographical/literary information (Chapters 7, 5) will offer complementary perspectives to your reports. Finally, we will show how to cite and evaluate any or all of these sources before you incorporate them into your written or oral reports (Chapters 7, 9).

Types of questions

Now that you are in the library with a map, chances are that you have a series of questions to clarify. This is a good starting point in library research. Figure 1.8 gives examples of two types of questions you might have.

What kind of information? Examples:

- Book (play, movie) reviews
- Addresses of people, schools, political representatives
- Books on global warming
- Portrait of an artist (e.g., Vincent van Gogh)

How much information? Examples:

- An overview article about the Declaration of Independence
- Best or most recent books on American short story writers

Figure 1.8: Types of questions to ask

One class of questions, "kind of information," will lead you to the appropriate type of reference source. For example, in the book review example, you will find reviews in newspapers (e.g., *Los Angeles Times*; *New York Times*, *New York Review of Books* at <http://www.nybooks.com/nyrev/index.html>); in larger libraries, and especially college libraries, you will want to find excerpts from reviewing sources in one place. Use the *Book Review Digest* and look first under the author's name in the author index.

The other class of questions, "how much information", is equally important. For an overview article about the Declaration of Independence, a seventh grade student might be happy with an encyclopedia article (e.g., from W*orld Book Encyclopedia*) and books; bibliographies, primary sources, or magazine articles on the subject might be more appropriate for a twelfth grade student.

Characteristics of reference sources

Figure 1.9 outlines various categories of reference sources based on five characteristics: type, time, format, medium, and detail. We can use these characteristics in selecting the ideal reference source. Each of these five categories is described and illustrated shortly. As Figure 1.9 shows, by type of reference sources, you can select between factual sources, such as dictionaries, encyclopedias, and almanacs, and bibliographic sources, such as library catalogs and bibliographies (TYPE). In addition, some reference sources will give you current events, while others will include historical perspective only (TIME).

Some sources will be mainly text-oriented, while others will contain graphics (FORMAT). While some sources are printed, others will include sound, animation, and other interactive features (MEDIUM). Finally, some sources will be simpler to use than others that have more detail and information (DETAIL).

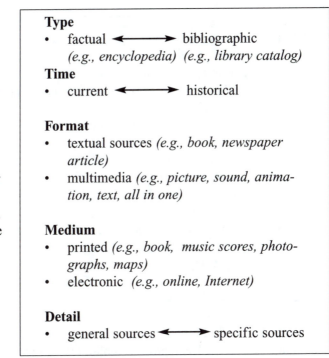

Type
- factual ⟷ bibliographic
  (e.g., encyclopedia) (e.g., library catalog)

Time
- current ⟷ historical

Format
- textual sources *(e.g., book, newspaper article)*
- multimedia *(e.g., picture, sound, animation, text, all in one)*

Medium
- printed *(e.g., book, music scores, photographs, maps)*
- electronic *(e.g., online, Internet)*

Detail
- general sources ⟷ specific sources

Figure 1.9: Characteristics of reference sources

Types of reference sources

There are two main types of reference sources (see Figure 1.10):

- Factual sources typically provide facts, such as the meaning of a word, the telephone number of your local pharmacy, a street map, a description of an actor's works, a baseball legend, a human rights activist. Examples of factual sources are dictionaries, directories, almanacs, handbooks, and yearbooks. Some dictionaries and encyclopedias offer brief references. For example, many articles in *The New Grove Dictionary of Music and Musicians* contain bibliographies for further reading. The same is true for many in-depth encyclopedias, such as *World Book Encyclopedia* and *Encyclopedia Britannica*.

- Bibliographic sources, on the other hand, provide bibliographic references or citations to books and articles. Library catalogs identify and describe the library's items by means of giving the author's name, title, publisher, and date. Online magazine databases describe individual articles that appear in magazines and newspapers. An example is *ProQuest* at: <http://proquest.umi.com/> (Figure 1.10).

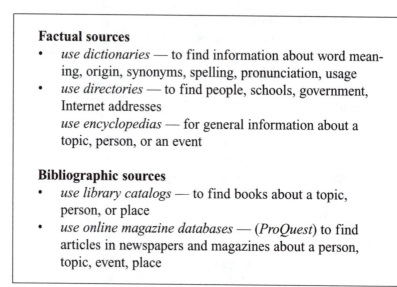

Factual sources

- *use dictionaries* — to find information about word meaning, origin, synonyms, spelling, pronunciation, usage
- *use directories* — to find people, schools, government, Internet addresses

  use encyclopedias — for general information about a topic, person, or an event

Bibliographic sources

- *use library catalogs* — to find books about a topic, person, or place
- *use online magazine databases* — (*ProQuest*) to find articles in newspapers and magazines about a person, topic, event, place

Figure 1.10: Types of reference sources

At the heart of all bibliographic sources is the bibliographic record. The example in Figure 1.11 is typical of bibliographic records in library catalogs.

Author:	Latour, Bruno
Title:	Laboratory life : the construction of scientific facts / Bruno Latour, Steve Woolgar ; introduction by Jonas Salk ; with a new postscript and index by the authors.
Published:	Princeton, N.J.: Princeton University Press, c1986.
Description:	294 p. : ill. ; 22 cm.
Subjects:	Biology—Research. Biology—Methodology.

Figure 1.11: Bibliographic record

The record gives the author's name (Bruno Latour), title (Laboratory life), publication date (1986), as well as subject matter (Biology—Research; and Biology—Methodology).

You also know the number of pages that the book contains, if it is illustrated, and its size. Note that the introduction is written by Jonas Salk. An important feature of this book is an index that was created by the authors themselves.

EXERCISE 1.1: Search for books on early American history

Search your (online) library catalog for books on early American history (the colonial period, 1600-1775). Answer the following questions:

1. What did you type in?

2. How many books did you find?

3. How many books did you locate (physically) in your library?

Time of sources

Time as a characteristic of information sources is important and will be used (see Figure 1.12):

1. To limit search to a desired time: most recent articles on civil rights; current research on DNA.
2. To ask a specific question, "how are anxiety disorders currently treated".

Chances are that you will need to read current books only. So if your search matches hundreds of items on civil rights, you might want to limit to a particular year. By selecting a specific time period, your search result will be more focused. Consider the following questions.

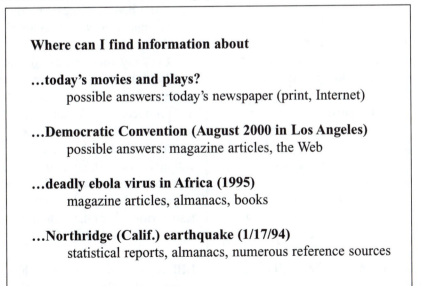

Where can I find information about

...today's movies and plays?
    possible answers: today's newspaper (print, Internet)

...Democratic Convention (August 2000 in Los Angeles)
    possible answers: magazine articles, the Web

...deadly ebola virus in Africa (1995)
    magazine articles, almanacs, books

...Northridge (Calif.) earthquake (1/17/94)
    statistical reports, almanacs, numerous reference sources

Figure 1.12: Time as a characteristic of reference sources

For current information that has not been printed in magazine articles, chances are that you will find plenty in the news and on the Internet; here's how:

<http://www.PAPERNAME.com/>   where PAPERNAME is replaced by the actual title of a newspaper:

Examples:
<http://www.nytimes.com/>
<http://www.infoworld.com/>
<http://www.latimes.com/>
<http://www.elpais.es/>

If you are prepared to wait longer for journal articles, books, and encyclopedia articles, chances are that the writing will be less current but well researched and peer-reviewed by the scholarly community. You will also have a wider choice of sources to select from. So, the further you are removed from a specific date, the more sources will be available to you. Published sources in established journals will be more scholarly in nature, will be peer-reviewed, will have bibliographies, and should be more reliable and valid. This process is time consuming and may take up to one year or more to complete. This means that you may have to wait longer for a book to be published than for a newspaper article to be printed. The price for this quality: time.

Format of sources

Information may be represented in many different formats. Include information from books, atlases, photographs, manuscripts, and other texts (see Figure 1.13).

Let's say you write an illustrated children's book. The content is represented in the form of a book. A TV producer comes along and decides that the content of that book would be ideal for her new TV educational series. She uses text, animation and audio, based on the content of your book. Your ideas are being transformed from the BOOK form to the MOVING PICTURE form.

Different formats are available in most libraries. Do not limit yourself to books, or any other single format.

Book-like publications
- books, anthologies, atlases

Cartographic publications
- maps, aerial photographs

Sound recordings
- tapes, compact discs

Pictures
- still images, movies

Multimedia
- graphics, animation, audio, text, all in one document (e.g., Internet)

Figure 1.13: Format as a characteristic of reference sources

Same content — different media

Just about any reference source can appear in a variety of media — another characteristic of information sources. The same content may be packaged as a printed book, as a computer database, and on the Internet.

EXERCISE 1.2: Printed versus Internet version of the same content

In order to get a feel for some of the differences between printed and electronic media, try using the following source: *Encyclopedia Britannica* <http://www.eb.com/> and its multi-volume printed version. Search for information on Thomas Jefferson. Compare and contrast these two versions and answer the following questions:

1. Which of the two versions (printed, Web) was easier for you to use and why?

2. Which version was faster to find the desired information?

3. Which version of the Encyclopedia Britannica was more interesting to use; explain why?

4. Comment on the general structure, hyperlinks, and the use of navigational buttons.

5. Does the Web page lead you to "further readings" and other useful links?

Level of detail

Level of detail is another characteristic of information sources. By "level of detail", we mean that not all sources will be of equal specificity, length, and scope. An article in *World Book Encyclopedia* on Nat Turner may give you just enough information to get you started in right direction. Another source might give you more detail, more facts, more leads to find further readings on your own, and so forth.

If you are exploring an area of human rights, the following general sources may be helpful as a starting point in your library search:

1. **Encyclopedias & handbooks:** *World Book Encyclopedia*; *Encyclopedia Britannica*; more specific titles will be found in larger libraries; an example is *Encyclopedia of Human Rights*.
2. **Library catalogs:** check library catalogs for books on civil rights. Trace specific political figures who significantly contributed to the civil rights movement in the 1960s.
3. **Online magazine databases:** *ProQuest* and *NewsBank*. More specific sources will be mentioned in Chapter 7.

Asking a good question or shaping a topic for your term-paper

Let us say, your teacher has given you the opportunity to choose a topic that interests you and then to write a paper on it. The best advice is to choose something that is intriguing and that you want to learn more about. The following cookbook technique will work in most cases. Many of the points we have discussed thus far may also be applied to defining a paper topic.

Start with a general topic: health, global change, music, Benjamin Franklin.

Apply any of the information characteristics on the general topic: another topic, time, a particular publication form, or location.

Example: health

There are many documents written on various aspects of health. You need to narrow down this general topic. Here is how:

    (a) add a subtopic (example: health and fitness among teenagers)
    (b) geographic area (example: United States)
    (c) publication formats (example: magazine articles, almanacs, Internet)
    (d) time, language (example: last 10 years in English)

Your working topic might be as follows:

> Identify sources published within last 10 years that discuss trends of health and fitness among teenagers in the United States.

To get some practice, use the template given below. The template is divided into 3 parts. The first part is reserved for a general topic. The second part contains some of the characteristics that we introduced earlier. In the third part, include the specific title for your term paper.

Part 1. Your general topic: (example: Thomas S. Hutchinson, 1711–1780; you may substitute any other historical figure, such as Paul Revere, Samuel Adams)

Part 2. Narrow down your general topic by using any or all of the following characteristics

    (a) subtopic (example: U.S. politics and government up to 1775 — Colonial period)
    (b) geographic area (example: Massachusetts)
    (c) publication format (example: books, atlases, portraits)
    (d) time and language, when appropriate (example: most recent English documents)
    (e) medium (example: printed, selected Internet sources)

Part 3. Your focused topic: **English language books and atlases published recently on the impact Thomas Hutchinson had on the causes of American Revolution; information in printed sources is preferred.**

You can work out several examples using this template. Select topics from history, sciences, the arts, and other subject matters. See **Think Guide for Chapter 1** at the end of this Chapter for more examples on how to narrow down a topic.

What you have learned

In Chapter 1 we have learned that there is a wide variety of sources that you can explore and use in your work. They differ by type, time, format, medium, and level of detail. Different sources are organized differently. They are searched differently, too. The Chapter presented a roadmap (Figure 1.7) and suggests a sequence of sources that you might find useful in your research. You do not have to always start with encyclopedias, but these sources are helpful starting points, especially if you are exploring a topic. This Chapter is also introducing some basic terms and concepts that you will find throughout this book.

You learned that asking a good question, or focusing your term paper is important. Several examples illustrate how a fairly general topic can be narrowed down so that it is manageable in your research effort. In addition, Think Guide for Chapter 1 following this Chapter provides space for you to practice and master this research skill.

Finally, planning library research early on is important for thorough and efficient work. Here, you may use a well-known analogy. If you want to watch an important sport event, you need to make plans well in advance: make sure that you are free that day, buy tickets, and coordinate with your friends. Library research takes time and planning is critical.

Now you can think about your term-papers the way most experts do. They break down their research activity into smaller parts; design an overall plan; ask questions:

- Which types of sources are the first best sources?

- Do I have to visit other libraries?

- If the library borrows an item from another library through an inter-library loan service, how much time will it take before I actually get that item?

Finally, you gather information; you will most likely modify your initial interest because, in the process, you learned and asked good questions. Researching is not a linear process; it goes through many loops, spirals, dips, and uneven learning curves. Most of the time, however, library research and exploration are rewarding activities.

Think Guide for Chapter 1: Topic Narrowing Exercise

Introduction to the teachers and media specialists: The topic-narrowing guide has two parts. We will first show a worked out example; then you will find a blank form so that you can use it with your students. This form is the extension of the section "Asking a good question or shaping a topic for your term-paper" in Chapter 1. It can work well both for imposed questions and student-generated questions. Typically, students will work on teacher assigned projects.

Getting started right. Students will be asked to write a paper, present their work in class, prepare some type of visual (poster, chart, brochure, model, diorama), or to work on assignments on a given topic. The topic here is taken broadly, to include people, places, events, processes, timelines, materials, and concepts. Students will approach their assignments differently, depending on their familiarity with the topic, their grade level, the subject matter, and the final format of the project.

A narrowing down exercise requires a mix of cognitive demands on students, including collaboration in small teams, communication skills, learning new concepts, connecting to known concepts, problem solving techniques, and so forth.

What follows is a general think guide that will help students focus or narrow down their topic.

Example: Topic narrowing described and annotated

Larger topics (to Roman Empire): ancient civilizations → civilizations → history/art/classics

This means that if you searched under "ancient civilizations", your books and other publications may be on any known civilization: Egypt, China, Greece, Rome, Persia, and not just on the Roman Empire.

> **Assigned topic**
> "Roman Empire"

Also known as ancient Rome, Latin civilization (you may also use these words to search material on the Roman Empire)

Smaller topics (to Roman Empire): students may use any of the following words to narrow down their general topic of Roman Empire, such as Roman laws; Roman gods. The list below is not arranged in any particular order. Ask the students to cluster similar words together and show, if possible, how various words and clusters are related to one another.

> army; vessels, navy; sieges and campaigns;
> emperors; specific emperors (Caesar, Augustus); citizens;
> temples, baths, arches, aqueducts; the Forum; gardens;
> gods; religion
> laws;
> literature; the arts; architecture; cities (Pompeii, Herculaneum);
> administration; colonies;
> slavery; types of gladiators; freedman;
> education;
> family; children, women, costumes; homes; meals;
> courtship, marriage;
> sickness, healing, medicine;
> death; excavation

time: 510 B.C. - 476 A.D.

place: Rome, Italy, Mediterranean

types of sources: printed, electronic, Web-based encyclopedias, books, pictures, maps

Exercise: Topic narrowing

Larger topics (than assigned):

```
                        Assigned topic


```

also known as:

Smaller topics (to assigned topic):

```



```

time:

place:

types of sources:

CHAPTER 2

Finding
Search Words

In this chapter you will learn:
1. To search library collections by using "subject headings"
2. To differentiate between subject headings and keywords
3. To use the power of a classification system — Dewey Decimal Classification System

This chapter focuses on important tools which will help you in searching publications by what they are about. In other words, we want to spend some time on the many ways we can search library material by subject. The tools that you will use in the process of collecting such material include the subject headings from Library of Congress Subject Headings (LCSH) and the main classes from Dewey Decimal Classification (DDC). For details on DDC class subdivisions, see **Appendix A** in back of this book. For extensive illustrations and tips, see **Think Guide for Chapter 2** in back of this Chapter.

How do we access publications?
There are two main approaches to searching library publications: by knowing the name of an author (creator) and/or title ("known-item search"); and by knowing the subject matter of a desired publication ("subject search"). This chapter, as noted earlier, will show you how to search library objects such as books, maps, and other items according to their subject matter.

Suppose that the book in your hands has the following information: the author is Mark Twain; the title is *Adventures of Huckleberry Finn*; other items of interest might be that the book was published in 1996 by Random House in New York. Using some of these data, how would you search the book to find out if there is another copy somewhere in your library? You are probably guessing correctly. You would search by the author's name, *mark twain*, and the title of the publication, *adventures of huckleberry finn*. This is why this type of search is called a known-item search. As a result of your search, you would see a library catalog entry like the one in Figure 2.1.

Author: Twain, Mark, 1835–1910.
Title: Adventures of Huckleberry Finn / Mark Twain; introduction by Justin Kaplan ; foreword and addendum by Victor Doyno.
Edition: 1st ed.
Published: New York : Random House, ©1996.
Description: xxviii, 418 p. : ill. ; 25 cm.
Subject(s): Finn, Huckleberry (Fictitious character)—Fiction.
Boys—Travel—Mississippi River—Fiction.
Boys—Missouri—Fiction.

Call number: FIC TWA 1996

Figure 2.1: Cataloging entry

However, if you did not know either the name of the author or the title of the book, you would probably try to search by subject. If you were to search this book by subject, how would you do it? Surely, from the example above, you might just look at the subject headings, labeled "Subject(s)," that are assigned to the book to find if the library has more books on the same or similar topics. Depending how much you know about Twain's *Adventures*, you could search by means of the following headings:

Authors, American—19th century.
Authors, American—19th century—Biography.
Boys—Travel—Mississippi River—Fiction.
Boys—Missouri—Fiction.
Finn, Huckleberry (Fictitious character)—Fiction.
Mississippi River—Description and travel.
Mississippi River—Fiction.
Mississippi River Valley—Social life and customs.
Twain, Mark, 1835-1910—Journeys—Mississippi River Valley.

Figure 2.2: Library of Congress Subject Headings (LCSH)

To help you find useful subject headings that are effective in your searching, there are published lists of subject headings. One of them is a list created by the Library of Congress which was initially used to describe subject matter of materials at the Library of Congress; hence, the name Library of Congress

Subject Headings (LCSH). Nowadays, it is used in most American libraries to describe books by their subject matter. Some specialized subject vocabularies are on the Web. An example is Getty's Art & Architecture Thesaurus at <http://www.getty.edu/research/tods/vocabularies/aat/>. You may want to visit their vocabulary site and search for words and phrases on any art and architecture object or concept (e.g., gardens; impressionism).

Getting started: An introduction to LCSH

If you were to search books on "homelessness", which among the following words or phrases would you select?

homeless people	social work with the homeless
homeless children	writings of the homeless persons
homeless veterans	underground homeless persons
homelessness	homeless youth
camps for the homeless	homeless youth in berkeley, california
homeless age	shelters for the homeless

Figure 2.3: Possible subject headings for books on "homelessness"

Some of the questions you might ask are: where do I find these words and phrases? Do I need to use all of them in searching library material? Which ones are the most useful? Do I use plural or singular, which order do I type the multi-word phrases? These are all good questions because, whenever you search computer catalogs for books, you will be searching with words and phrases. Recall our roadmap chart from Chapter 1 (Figure 1.7). You will notice that Library of Congress Subject Headings (LCSH) play an important role in the search process. Most importantly, subject headings are used to find accurate and complete search words under which to look up books in library catalogs.

As an optional exercise, visit your library and ask for the volumes of LCSH "red books". You will find the most current edition of LCSH books in the reference area, near the reference desk. In many school libraries, these books may be held in back and used by people who catalog books. Suppose you wish to find books on missions. Try to find headings related to missions in LCSH. What you probably find is an alphabetical list of headings related to various kinds of missions as well as a particular type of notation similar to the one shown on the next page.

Catholic Church—Missions
NT (narrower term) Catholic Church—Missions—Pictorial works
Faith missions movement
Mission buildings, Spanish
     USE Spanish mission buildings
Spanish missions buildings—United States
Spanish mission buildings in art

RT (related term) to the "Spanish mission buildings in art" is:

Architecture, Domestic—Mission style

Figure 2.4: Subject headings (LCSH) related to "missions"

Look up the following headings in LCSH: Boston Massacre; Boston Tea Party; Boston Colonial period; speeches; heavy metal; energy; oxygen; Aztec civilization; Nicaragua—Social conditions.

We summarize here what you may have already discovered on your own. We can use LCSH as a dictionary that gives you words, synonyms, and definitions. As in the example above, the reader is directed to USE Spanish mission buildings rather than Mission buildings, Spanish. More importantly, LCSH may be thought of as a navigational tool that shows the types of relationships that exist between and among subject headings. For example, if you searched under Catholic Church—Missions and retrieved too many items, you might want to search under more specific terms, such as Catholic Church—Missions—Pictorial works. Typically the more specific terms are labeled as "narrower terms" (NT). See Figure 2.5.

On the other hand, if your search produced only a few documents, you could expand your search by using "broader terms" (BT) and "related terms" (RT). For example, in the excerpt on missions, the related heading is Architecture, Domestic—Mission style.

To give you more time to practice, consider the following excerpt from LCSH on the topic of COOKERY. In Figure 2.5, the instruction in the parentheses, "May Subd Geog," means that you can search material on, for example, cookery in various geographical locations (e.g., Brazil, Spain, Japan).

Cookery is preferred term ——→	**Cookery** (May Subd Geog)
Cuisine is *not* to be used ——→	UF Cuisine
Broader Term ——→	BT Home economics
Related Term to cookery ——→	RT Dinners and dining
Narrower Terms ——→	NT Appetizers
	Baking
	Boiling (Cookery)
	Braising (Cookery)
	Brunches
	Buffets (Cookery)
	Canning and preserving
	Carving (Meats, etc.)
	Casserole cookery
	Chafing dish cookery
	Complex carbohydrate diet—Recipes
	Confectionery
	Cookery (Butterscotch)
	Cookery (Natural foods)…
	Fireplace cookery
	Food—Effect of heat on
	Food presentation
	High-calcium diet—Recipes
	High-carbohydrate diet—Recipes
	High-fiber diet—Recipes
	Holiday cookery
	Low budget cookery
	Low-calorie diet—Recipes
	Low-cholesterol diet—Recipes
	Outdoor cookery
	Quick and easy cookery
	Salt-free diet—Recipes
	Sandwiches
	Solar cookery
	Stews
	Sugar-free diet—Recipes
	Tempura
	Vegetarian cookery
	Cookery, American—California style…
	Cookery (Blueberries)…
	Cookery (Dandelions)…

Figure 2.5: Excerpt from LCSH on Cookery

EXERCISE 2.1: Questions related to LCSH

Using the LCSH example on the next page, please answer the following questions.

1. Looking at the cookery headings in Figure 2.5, can you search for books on fat-free diets?
   ❏ Yes   ❏ No

2. If not, what would be an appropriate subject heading to search under?

3. Still referring to Figure 2.5, can you search for publications under Cookery, Cook Islands?
   ❏ Yes   ❏ No

4. Can you recommend to your friend a correct phrase to look up for books on California style, American cookery?

To summarize, LCSH is designed to:

1. Control terms and phrases that are spelled the same but may have different meanings, also known as homonyms (e.g., mercury—heavy metal, planet, goddess; heavy metals—toxic metals such as arsenic, nickel, and lead; rock group; pitch—aeronautics, music, baseball; plant—botany, factory; SARA—baked products, Superfund Act). Homonyms are controlled with a definition of a preferred term or phrase.
2. Link terms and phrases that are spelled differently but mean the same, also known as synonyms (e.g., United States, US, USA; labour *see* labor; scientific name, *see* common name—sucrose *see* table sugar). Synonymous relationships are controlled with the USE and USED FOR (UF) reference notes.
3. Show a hierarchical relationship between and among terms and phrases (e.g., broader term (BT)—*buildings* is broader to *art deco buildings*; narrower term (NT)—*Cape Cod crystal* is narrower to *crystal*, and other relationships such as related terms (RT)—*birds* is related to *ornithology*).

EXERCISE 2.2: Subject headings from different perspectives

1. For books on **rock music**, especially in California, which subject headings would you use? Consult the LCSH books in your library or ask your librarian.

2. Does your library have any books on **heavy metal** in the context of music rather than metallurgy? Again, turn to LCSH books and look up alphabetically. Any headings that you may use in searching your library catalog?

Last word

You are probably wondering how the different elements are put together in a multi-word subject heading. These different elements are typically in the order of: Topic; Place; Time; Form. You do not have to have all of these elements in a single heading. The word "form" refers to different literary genres, such as biographies, bird's-eye views, cartoons, criticism, drama, fiction, or poetry. Music forms may include an aria, concerto, opera, sonata, or a song.

For example, the heading **Boston Massacre, 1770**, has the main topic (Boston Massacre) and date (1770). What can you say about the following headings in Figure 2.6?

Low-fat diet—Recipes.
Engraved glass—Europe—18th century.
Boston Tea Party, 1773.
France—Intellectual life—20th century—Historiography.

Figure 2.6: Order of subject words in subject headings

Other ways of searching by subject

■ There are several indirect ways to search library material by what they are about without using subject headings. For example, once you discover that a certain author specializes on a particular topic or subtopic, you might do the **author search** to obtain his or her bibliography; display several records and look at the subject headings. Use those headings in your subsequent searches to retrieve more books on the same or similar topics. You can also extend this search technique and search the Web under the author's name.

■ Another way to search library material by their subject matter is by a known **series title**. For example, to obtain a broad collection of writings on various controversial subjects (e.g., gun control, euthanasia, affirmative action, homosexuals in the military, capital punishment), search under *library of american biography*; another search might be on *opposing viewpoints*. What you will retrieve will be books with different titles and on different controversial topics; however, all of these books will be within the same series title: opposing viewpoints.

■ Probably, the most common way that people search is by means of **keywords**; the keyword approach typically gives a broad retrieval because the computer matches your words against all subject-rich words (from titles, series titles, subject headings, table of contents, notes). However, keywords are not controlled in any way. In particular,
  • homonyms are not controlled (e.g., "heavy metals" may retrieve a rock group by that name, not items on cadmium and nickel; the word "seals" may have different meanings: animals, law, numismatics);
  • synonyms are not linked (e.g., material on lead may be scattered under lead, pb, toxic substances).

This is the basic difference between searching library catalogs and Internet resources. Library materials can be searched in a variety of ways; the Internet, at the moment, is mainly a keyword search.

Classification system

In contrast to scientific classifications (e.g., biological taxonomy), library classifications organize writings by their topics. Examples of classification systems are: Dewey Decimal Classification (DDC) and Library of Congress Classification (LCC). For DDC subdivisions, see Appendix A.

The ten main classes in Dewey Decimal Classification are:

- **000 generalities** — computer science, dictionaries & encyclopedias, museums
- **100 philosophy & psychology** — ethics, logic
- **200 religion** — Christianity, Islam, Judaism, Buddhism
- **300 social sciences** — politics, government, gender studies, education
- **400 language** — language groups, linguistics excluding the literature
- **500 natural sciences** — astronomy, physics, chemistry, biology & mathematics
- **600 technology**— applied sciences including medicine, engineering, cooking
- **700 the arts**—fine and decorative arts: music, cinema, visual arts, architecture
- **800 literature & rhetoric** — literatures of different languages
- **900 geography & history** — books on the general history of U.S. go under 973

To explore subdivisions of these ten classes of the Dewey Decimal Classification, visit the Internet Public Library site at: <http://www.ipl.org/youth/dewey/>.

EXERCISE 2.3: Questions related to the Dewey Decimal Classification

Using the main DDC classes, answer the following questions.

1. Find the general area in your library where the books on the **United States presidents** are shelved. What is the general Dewey Decimal class that contains these books?

2. Search for books on the **United States history colonial period (ca. 1600-1775)**. Which general class is given to books on this topic?

Bonus point:
3. Where would you find current music encyclopedias?

The power of call numbers

To the users of libraries, classification is an important tool which brings together in one place (collocates) books on the same or similar topics; it also facilitates browsing which is an important exploratory technique. Each numeral and character has an important meaning. In fact, some librarians can tell you what a book is about just by looking at the call number. For example, your librarian will know that the material in the class 510 will be on the general topic of mathematics; that books in the division 516 are on geometry; and that the Euclidean geometry books will be in the 516.2 subdivision.

Since one of the purposes of a classification system is to facilitate the browsing of books in library stacks, you can use Dewey Decimal Classification (DDC) to find more useful books. Here is how. If you already found four books on your topic and need more like those that you have, try the following:

1. Notice that all your books on the general history of the United States have call numbers starting with the number "973."
2. Go to the library stacks; browse the area around the books that you have found useful.
3. Select additional books that you consider relevant by scanning their title, table of contents, index, preface, randomly picked pages, pictures.
4. Search these books in the library catalog; find the subject headings for these additional books. Use these subject headings in your subsequent searches.

What you have learned

Chapter 2 concentrates on the various approaches to subject searching. In particular, we introduce the importance of the Library of Congress Subject Headings (LCSH), its notation, and the various ways to use LCSH in searching library catalogs. The Chapter also introduces you to the concept of classification, and in particular, to the Dewey Decimal Classification System. The power of call numbers is illustrated.

This chapter has introduced the following terms and concepts. We define the main vocabulary.

Call number	Unique identification number assigned to each library item. A book on Chicano rock music by David Reyes will uniquely be identified by its call number 781.66 REY.
Dewey Decimal Classification System	DDC classifies books and book-like publications into 10 main classes (e.g., books on "music" will be grouped in class 780; general math books go under

class 510). DDC groups together items on the same or similar topics. It also facilitates browsing of items on shelves.

Library of Congress Subject Headings (LCSH)   LCSH is a vocabulary designed to control homonyms, synonyms, and assist you in searching for broader and narrower topics. It also suggests related subject headings to the ones you used. Subject headings are controlled search terms used to find accurate and complete subjects under which to look up books in library catalogs. These can be single words (e.g., Cookery) or multi-word phrases (e.g., Massachusetts—History—Colonial period.—ca. 1600–1775).

Think Guide for Chapter 2: Finding Search Words

Introduction to teachers and media specialists: Once the students have been assigned projects and have a general research plan, they will start to think about specific words and phrases that they will use in searching encyclopedias, library catalogs, and magazine databases. Where do they find the "right" words? Think Guide for Chapter 2 is designed to save students' time and improve their skills.

The best sources for finding the "right" words are encyclopedias, textbooks, some dictionaries, and the library vocabulary that we discussed earlier in Chapter 2, **Library of Congress Subject Headings**. The rule of thumb is that the more students know about a topic they are searching on, the more successful they will be in finding the "right" vocabulary. In addition, imagination helps.

Hints that will save time and improve students' skills

Think of a topic that includes your topic.
Example: your topic is BASKETBALL; the topics that include this topic are ball sports, team sports, and sports, in general. These topics are **broader** than the one you are searching on.

Think of a topic that is:
    A part of your topic;   ⟵   all these words will be more
    A member of your topic;   specific than your topic
    That your topic is divided into;
    That your topic consists of.
Example: your topic is still basketball; the subtopic that is a part of basketball is basketball teams, players, coaches, basketball competitions, championships, strategies, etc. These topics are **narrower** or more specific than the topic you are searching on.

Think of a variant topic (word-order) such as
    Spelling variation;
    Popular name:
    Dialect of;
    Point-of-view.
These are **synonymous** terms. Good sources for finding the "right" words and synonyms and antonyms are the *Library of Congress Subject Headings* (an excellent source for basketball) and *Roget's Thesaurus*.

Example #1: Finding search words on basketball

We will start off by giving you two examples under the heading, athletics; the topics are: **basketball**, and the **Olympic Games 2000**. The assigned topics appear in a box. Words above the box are more general topics than basketball; words and phrases below basketball are narrower. The effect will be that there will be more material on the broader topics than on the more specific ones. For example, you will find more books in your library on the general topic of SPORTS than on, basketball alone, or on the NBA, LA's Lakers, Shaq, Indiana's Pacers, and so on.

The example below consists of our own words and depends on how much we know about BASKETBALL; this author's knowledge about ball games is limited, so she does not have an extensive vocabulary in this area. If you were a basketball coach or a fan, chances are that your vocabulary would be more elaborate. For the purposes of comparison, compare the vocabulary below with the LCSH on basketball.

Sports	Use dictionaries to define the meaning of the word "sports" You may find different words that people use to mean sports, such as athletics, games.
Team sports	Find out which sports are called "team sports" Write down several examples of team sports; is diving a team sport (archery, swimming, water polo, tae kwon do, track-and-field)?
Basketball	Find rules, timeline and how it started; find statistical information. Learn about similar sports such as volleyball, handball, soccer, water polo.

— Competitions (world, national, local); the Olympics; Special Olympics
    — Professional team competition versus college team competition
        — NBA championships
            — NBA championship 2000 (Los Angeles)
                — Lakers (LA team)
                — Phil Jackson, coach
                — Shaq (Shaquille O'Neil), Kobe Bryant, etc.

Example #2: Finding search words on Olympic Games

The Olympic Games

Athletics
    Competitive Athletics
        The Olympic Games (also known as Olympics)
           Summer, Winter
           Special Olympics

The Olympic Games 2000	Sydney Harbor

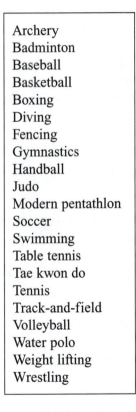

Archery
Badminton
Baseball
Basketball
Boxing
Diving
Fencing
Gymnastics
Handball
Judo
Modern pentathlon
Soccer
Swimming
Table tennis
Tae kwon do
Tennis
Track-and-field
Volleyball
Water polo
Weight lifting
Wrestling

Sydney Olympic Park

Exercise: Finding the right words on your own

Think of larger topics that might include the one you are trying to understand.

Does it fall into history, geography, philosophy, civics, the sciences, the arts, many different interrelated topics (often called interdisciplinary)? If so, is there a predominant topic?

Is your topic predominantly about:

You will find it in the following sources

■ **IDEAS**
encyclopedias, books, selected Web sites
Check for definitions, overview, biases, references

■ **PEOPLE**
encyclopedias, biographical dictionaries, books, the Web
Check for name spelling, name variations, time and place, contributions

■ **PLACES**
maps, atlases, the Web, encyclopedias, almanacs, books
Check for variations in place names, sources of compilation (governments, scholarly societies)

■ **UNKNOWN WORDS**
dictionaries, encyclopedias (check for spelling, synonyms)

How much do you already know about your topic?

If nothing or little, find an article in an encyclopedia, your textbook, library book and follow the road map from Chapter 1, Figure 1.7.

Think of smaller (narrower, more specific) topics that might be part of your topic. See our example of TYPES OF Olympic Games (from archery to wrestling).

■ List all subtopics that might be a type of, or part of your topic.

■ Cluster subtopics that are similar into individual classes, like all team sports together.

At first, finding the right words may seem to be difficult, however, with enough practice and familiarity with your topic, it becomes much easier. Remember, in the long run we're trying to make your search for information more efficient and effective.

CHAPTER 3

Search Strategies

In this chapter students will learn:
1. To plan their search by using various search strategies
2. To search library collections by using various subject approaches
3. To use Boolean operators (i.e., AND, OR, NOT) to connect concepts and search terms together
4. To modify search results: (a) expand search results (if few records are retrieved), and (b) narrow down search results (if too many records are retrieved)

This chapter focuses on the concept of "search strategy" as it relates to searching online library catalogs, magazine databases, or Web collections. A search strategy is defined as an overall plan for a search problem in order to achieve a particular goal. For example, if your goal is to write a paper about sports in Rome you need to have a strategy that would help you compile a list of publications on the topic of sports in Rome. Here are some examples of research topics:

■ Describe early American settlements and towns
■ Examine the early settlers and look at their former home countries
■ Report on the ways that historical figures such as John Hancock and Thomas Hutchinson shaped the development and growth of early American politics, government, and society
■ Explain natural phenomena such as the greenhouse effect
■ Find a pen-pal from Mexico or Japan and ask them about their favorite books, sports, holidays, and classes.

You will find answers to these questions in books, atlases, reference sources, magazine and newspaper articles as well as on the Internet. Regardless of the format and medium, you must cite each of these publications (see Chapter 9) and arrange them alphabetically by their authors' names or some other meaningful way. The result will be your own bibliography, an essential part of your research report or presentation. A *good* search strategy will produce a *good* bibliography.

Specifically, we will focus on identifying basic concepts, linking these concepts to one another, evaluating tentative results of your searches, and modifying the strategy. You will learn to:

1. Combine words (also known as terms) using basic operators to tell the system how to perform the search (we'll cover the main three operators AND, OR, and NOT, referred to as Boolean operators).
2. Construct search strategies.
3. Modify your search results — you will learn how to expand if you get too little; or to limit your search, if you get too much.

Once we gather search words (a time-consuming task itself; see Chapter 2), we are ready to link the terms with one another. There are many different ways to do so.

Often during the search process, you will modify your search strategy in order to increase or decrease the number of records.

Basic operators: AND

The example below is the use of the AND operator. It ANDs concept A ("toys") and concept B ("colonial america") and creates a set of documents in the shaded area or the intersection, where each document must deal both with the concept "TOYS" and the concept "COLONIAL AMERICA."

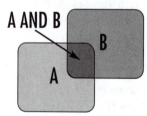

If you use concept A, which covers the topic of "toys" with 200 documents, and separately, concept B "colonial america" with 100 documents, the intersection of A and B might give you 40 documents. The effect of the AND operator is that it reduces the size of the retrieved set; this can be helpful if you initially obtain too many entries.

EXERCISE 3.1: Use of the AND operator

Search your library catalog for books on missions in California. First type in the word missions in your search box; observe the number of retrieved items. Make sure that the operator is switched to the AND operator. Type in the word california in a separate search box; observe the number of retrieved items. What is your conclusion?

OPTIONAL EXERCISE

Repeat this example in the Melvyl® library catalog <http://www.melvyl.ucop.edu>. Unlike your local library catalog that retrieves books that your school library has, Melvyl® provides access to many libraries in the state of California. Limit your search to a specific library, English language books, and to recent publications only. How many items did you find?

EXERCISE 3.2: Directed search for "team sport" in "US"

Suppose you are looking for material (e.g., books, magazine and newspaper articles) on team sports in the United States. Do the following:

1. Identify the most important concepts (example: **team sport; United States**)

2. Search each one separately in the library catalog (example: **team sports**)

3. Notice the number of results for each of these separate sets

4. Combine all sets; how many matches did you get?
   Example: **team sports** (AND) **united states** ⟶ number of records: _____

In this exercise, think of your research topic; for your topic, apply the instructions a through d.

Your topic:

    (a)   Identify the two most important concepts.
    (b)   Search each concept separately.
    (c)   Notice the number of results for each.
    (d)   Combine sets noting the number of matches.

Basic operators: OR

This type of operator, known as the OR operator, creates the union of at least two words. (An example is the union of two words, Lawyers or Attorneys; Soccer or Football). The union creates a set of entries each of which deals with either term A (soccer) or term B (football) or both.

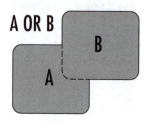

The effect of this operator is to broaden your search, so as to give you more records. Surely, by ORing more synonymous words, your set becomes larger. If you initially get too few items, you can add more synonymous terms to make your set larger.

EXERCISE 3.3: Design a search to be as complete as possible

You need to find material on early Colonies, or on the social conditions of Central American countries. How would you search so that the result is as complete as possible?

1. Which countries would you include?

2. Which operator would you use to broaden your search?

Basic operators: NOT

The NOT operator is a powerful operator which should be used with caution.

It allows you to eliminate all documents from your retrieval set that cover a topic that you DO NOT wish to retrieve. So, if you are not interested in documents that talk about "El Salvador," you can exclude them from your retrieval set. However, you need to be cautious because some of the docu-

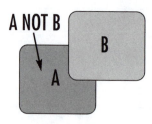

ments on El Salvador might be relevant to your general topic of "Central America." The same applies to another example: pollution. For example, if you do not exclude "air pollution," "noise pollution," and so on, you are likely to get books that contain information about these unwanted topics. So, in this context, the NOT operator is powerful yet requires caution.

EXERCISE 3.4: Use of the NOT operator

You are writing a paper on art glass.

1. How would you design your search so that the retrieved books discuss only art glass and not, for example, glass animals or glass sculpture?

2. You want to find material about Samuel Adams, and nothing on beer or breweries. What would your search look like?

3. In searching photography, you find many records that mention aerial photography. Since you already know about aerial photography, you decide to eliminate this term. How do you propose to do this search?

Search strategy

Search strategy refers to a set of instructions that can be understood by the system you search. The search strategy specifies search words (also known as search terms) and concepts as well as the logical relationship between and among them. You know where to find terms (see Chapter 2), and you have just learned about the three operators. We are ready to put terms and the logic together into various types of search strategies. We will start off with a "known-item" search.

■ **Known-item search** There are many reasons for using this type of search. For example, you want to verify an author's name, or to find the call number of a book recommended by your friend, or to locate it in your library, or see if it is even available. In all these cases, you sort of "know" the item you want, for example, the name of the author (artist, compiler, photographer) and/or title, and sometimes subject; this is the reason we call it a "known-item" search.

Another good reason to use the known-item search is to retrieve a record, and then use subject headings that are assigned to that record in order to obtain more entries. In the example of acid rain, you would retrieve records about acid rain. Then you would look up subject headings that the librarians assigned to this topic. Finally, you can use these subject headings in your subsequent searches to retrieve more of the same kind of material. Get the call numbers for these newly retrieved records. What do they have in common? Compare their subject headings. Compare their call numbers.

■ **Building block search** This type of search strategy, the "building block" strategy focuses on identifying "blocks" or your main concepts. This strategy is more systematic than the known-item search. Use paper and pencil to prepare in advance before you "go online." Here is how:

Step 1: Identify your main concepts ("blocks")

Step 2: Identify terms within each concept

Step 3: OR synonymous words within each separate block (or box)

Step 4: AND concepts horizontally

Step 5: Use paper and pencil before you "go online"

Step 6: Evaluate your options.

Suppose that your research paper is on *the history of team sports in the New England states*. The first thing you need to do is to identify distinct blocks: history; team sports; New England states. Next you need to list synonymous terms in each block. For example, the team sports block might include baseball, volleyball, football; the New England block might include individual states such as Rhode Island, Maine, Massachusetts, etc. It will save you a lot of time if you copy the template below for each search, at least in the beginning. For examples, see **Think Guide for Chapter 3** in back of this Chapter.

There should be a difference between the CONCEPTS and your WORDS. *Concepts* are used to represent important and discrete themes in your search. The concepts are ANDed across the template. *Words* are ORed within each of the concepts in the boxes below.

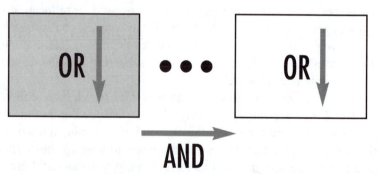

Modification: Broadening and narrowing down your search

Now is a good time to look at the search results, and assess your progress so far. You have learned useful techniques, but you want to improve your searching skills. There are several techniques that will improve your search results. This section focuses on two of these techniques: broadening and narrowing your search results.

Broadening your search strategy You will sometimes retrieve too few records. To get more, try the following four approaches:

1. By deleting an entire search BLOCK, you will increase your search considerably; delete the least useful block, the most generic block first; with each block deleted, you will have a fewer number of AND connectors.

2. By adding synonymous words within each of your blocks, you will again increase the size of your search set; add equivalent words (e.g., U.S., U.S.A, United States of America, North America) and then observe the number of results.

3. By adding broader words, you will see the difference in your search result.

4. Finally, you can truncate each of the concepts and words to further expand your search results. The word "truncate" means that you can sometimes search on the word root, such as law?. The symbol "?" will automatically search all words that match law or laws or lawful or lawyers. This feature depends on the source you are searching, such as the Web, online magazine databases, and library catalogs.

Narrowing your search strategy If you wish to get a smaller set of documents because you obtained too many initially, here are a few techniques to help you do so.

1. Add another concept; your result will decrease. Make sure you use an appropriate operator (i.e., AND, AND NOT).

2. Use specific words. For example, search under the word *baseball* rather than the word *sports*.

3. Along with main words, when possible and appropriate, include another topic, place, or specific format such as a map, book, or publication date.

Classify the following words or phrases into two separate groups so that you can combine these two groups with the AND operator.

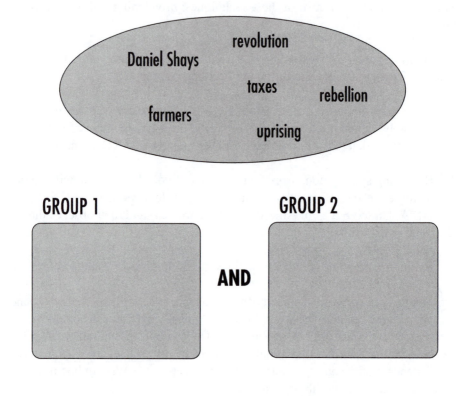

GROUP 1

GROUP 2

AND

What you have learned

In Chapter 3 you have learned how to create a step-by-step search strategy (or plan) by starting with a concept then narrowing or expanding the concept as necessary. This section glosses over the most important terms and concepts introduced in Chapter 3.

AND, OR, NOT operators
Each of these three operators is used in searching library material. They tell the system how to link search words. The AND operator narrows down your search; the OR operator broadens the search results; the NOT operator limits your search results.

Building-block search
Search strategy which identifies BLOCKS or main concepts of the search, and then combines the blocks using the operators and, or, not.

Known-item search
Search strategy that is often used to verify and locate documents in your library you know by author and/or title.

Modifying search
Uses operators with narrower and broader search words to focus or expand the search results.

Search strategy
A set of search instructions that are understood by the retrieval system you search.

Think Guide for Chapter 3: Search Strategies

Introduction to teachers and media specialists: Search strategy is described in Chapter 3 because it applies to any of the electronic sources that might be used in research projects: online library catalogs, electronic encyclopedias, online magazine and newspaper databases, as well as the Web. Search strategy has been traditionally included with online library catalogs and online magazine databases. However, as a brainstorming tool, it applies to all types of searching ranging from printed sources to the Web.

Under the general guidelines of curricular frameworks for high school students for grades 9–12 (NAEP), history/social science students are required to demonstrate (1) chronological and spatial thinking skills; (2) historical research, evidence and point of view; and (3) historical interpretation skills. This has direct implications for the design of information literacy programs. Among other things, it means that the students will learn to: (1) use multiple resources (e.g., textual, geographical, statistical in printed and electronic media); (2) differentiate between primary and secondary sources; (3) evaluate Web documents; (4) communicate, analyze, describe, classify, and apply information from selected sources to their projects.

> United States Department of Education. National Assessment Governing Board. (1998). *Civics framework for the 1998 National Assessment of Educational Progress, NAEP Civics*. Washington, D. C. : The Board. <http://www.nagb.org/>

An important part of searching techniques is the understanding how to combine search terms into various search strategies. Next, we show examples for the two types of search strategies that are used in most online systems.

Basic operators: AND The example below is the use of the AND operator. It ANDs concept A ("children") and concept B ("roman empire") and creates a set of documents in the shaded area or the *intersection*, where each document must deal both with the concept "CHILDREN" and the concept "ROMAN EMPIRE." The AND operator reduces the size of the retrieved set; this can be helpful if you initially obtain too many items.

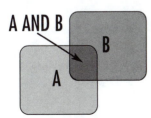

Basic operators: OR This type of operator, known as the OR operator, creates the union of at least two terms. An example is the union of two terms, "POMPEII" or "HERCULANEUM." The *union* creates a set of entries each of

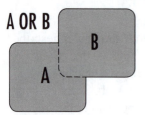

which deals with either term A (pompeii) or term B (herculaneum) or both. The effect of this operator is to broaden your search, so as to give you more items.

Example: Search strategies described and annotated

Putting Basic Operators Together: Put all words that represent a certain concept together in a single square; link them with an OR operator. Example: a single concept might be CITIES in the Roman Empire. "OR" all individual cities:

> rome OR pompeii OR herculaneum OR naples

Repeat with other concepts, such as ARCHITECTURE. "OR" all individual words and phrases that fall under the concept of architecture and put them in a single square. Example:

> forum OR baths OR temples OR arches OR gardens

Connect these two boxes with the AND operator. If you use this strategy to search library catalogs, the result will be books that talk about architectural objects (e.g., forums, baths, temples, arches, or gardens) in ancient cities such as Pompeii, Rome, Herculaneum, or Naples. If you use the same strategy to search online magazine databases, the result will be articles and reviews in magazines and journals on the same topic from current perspectives. Finally, you can apply the same strategy to search the Web. The result will be multimedia full documents with texts, pictures, maps, tables, flags, graphs, and so on. Take note of who wrote the document, the purpose it was written for, the date of writing, and the evidence presented!

Exercise: Search strategy

Put all words that represent a certain concept together in a single square; link them with an OR operator. If you have two different concepts, use two squares; for three concepts, add another square, and so forth. You get a picture.

Connect these squares with the AND operator.

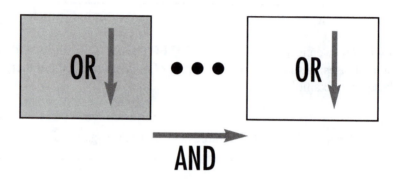

Fact Finding: Words, Concepts, Events, Places

In this chapter you will learn:
1. Differences between dictionaries and encyclopedias: uses, features, and types
2. Other fact finding sources: almanacs, directories, handbooks, and maps
3. Different types of dictionaries, encyclopedias, directories (e.g., print, Internet), and how to evaluate fact finding sources
4. Types of information needs which are suitable for dictionaries, encyclopedias, and other factual resources (e.g., almanacs, directories, handbooks, maps)

This chapter is divided into two sections: the first section focuses on dictionaries and encyclopedias; the second section covers other fact finding sources, also known as factbooks. These include almanacs, yearbooks, handbooks, directories, and geographical sources, such as maps, atlases and gazetteers. These sources contain specific pieces of information and often combine compilations of factual and statistical data about places, nations, persons, and events. You are probably familiar with some of the titles: *Bartlett's Familiar Quotations*, *Facts About the Presidents*, *Kane's Famous First Facts*, *The World Almanac and Book of Facts*, *Webster's New Geographical Dictionary*, or the *World Book Encyclopedia*.

Dictionaries and encyclopedias
This section discusses different types of dictionaries and encyclopedias, how to use them, and the way they fit into the larger picture of other reference

sources. You will see that many of the dictionaries and encyclopedias are becoming available on the Internet.

Different types of questions lead to different types of factbooks. Consider the following questions: where can I find . . . ?

1. An overview article about Thomas Jefferson.
2. Information about Boston (Massachusetts).
3. Rankings of liberal colleges in New York (or any state).
4. What is the favorite leisure activity in Brazil?

For example, to answer the first question, which type of reference source would be most suitable? Don't worry about specific titles in this exercise. (HINT: try *encyclopedias*).

Answers:

Question 2: (Boston) _____

Question 3: (liberal colleges)_____

Question 4: (leisure in Brazil)_____

Dictionaries defined

Dictionaries, also known as word books, have several meanings:

> **Dictionary** n., *pl.* -ies. [Med. Lat. *dictionarium* < Lat. *dictio*, diction.] 1. A reference book having an explanatory alphabetical list of words, with information given for each word, including meaning, pronunciation, etymology, and often usage guidance. 2. A book listing the words of a language with translations into another language. 3. A book listing linguistic items, as words, with specialized information about them <a legal *dictionary*> <a biographical *dictionary*> 4. Computer Sci. A list stored in machine-readable form for reference by an automatic system. (*Webster's II New Riverside University Dictionary*, 1984, p. 375)

This definition makes a distinction between several types of dictionaries: general language dictionaries (e.g., monolingual English language dictionaries); bi- and polyglot dictionaries (e.g., English-Spanish dictionaries, and those that list more than two languages); as well as specialized and technical dictionaries (e.g., *The New Grove Dictionary of Music and Musicians*; *Dictionary of the Environment*). Regardless of the type of dictionary, major elements in most dictionaries include: the definition of words, spelling and alternate spelling, word origin (etymology), usage, pronunciation, syllabification, grammatical information, synonyms, antonyms, homonyms, abbreviations, slang, places, people, events, and topics.

Characteristics of dictionaries

It is useful to think about dictionaries in terms of three main characteristics. With regard to **time**, there are current usage dictionaries that list contemporary language and slang as well as historical dictionaries that trace words to the earliest known usage. With regard to **medium** of implementation, there is a growing number of dictionaries that are available as printed books and on the Internet. Level of **detail** is another main characteristic that makes dictionaries so varied. Think of a topic and chances are that you will find dictionaries on a variety of specialized topics.

We begin with some dictionary titles that you probably recognize and use. Under the heading English language dictionaries, you will notice the following classes of dictionaries: "desk" or "college" dictionaries are typically one-volume English language dictionaries that will be sufficient for secondary schools. "Unabridged dictionaries" are typically large in size and scholarly in nature. We have listed two representative titles in this class of dictionaries. The *Oxford English Dictionary* (OED) is an example of a scholarly historical dictionary where each word is put in historical context and traced to the oldest known usage. You will be introduced to OED during your junior and senior years. Check your library bookshelf or your own home library. You might have one of these titles already.

■ Examples of English language general dictionaries are:
- **Desk or college dictionaries**
  American Heritage Dictionary of the English Language. 3rd ed.
       Boston: Houghton Mifflin, 1992.
  Webster's Ninth Collegiate Dictionary. Rev. ed. Springfield, Mass.:
       Merriam-Webster, 1990.
- **Unabridged (fully developed) dictionaries**
  Webster's Third New International Dictionary. Springfield, Mass.:
       Merriam-Webster, 1993. The Dictionary is a part of the Internet's
       version of the *Encyclopedia Britannica* at: <http://www.eb.com/>.
- **Etymological dictionary**
  The Oxford English Dictionary. J. A. Simpson and E. S. C. Weiner,
       eds. 2d ed. Oxford: Clarendon Press, 1989, 20 vols. Supplements.
- **Slang dictionaries**
  Chapman, Robert L., ed. *New Dictionary of American Slang.* New
       York: Harper & Collins, 1997.
  Partridge, Eric. *Dictionary of Slang and Unconventional English.* 1st
       American ed. New York: Macmillan, 1990.

- **Synonyms, Antonyms, Abbreviations**

  Roget's International Thesaurus. 5th ed. New York: HarperCollins, 1992. The Internet's version of *Roget's Thesaurus* is <http://www.thesaurus.com/>.

  Think of a word, say "abuse." Here is a two-step procedure for using the *Thesaurus.* Look up the word in the Index Guide in the back of the volume; notice a cluster of words (i.e., deceive 547.5; maltreat 649.7; misuse 679.2, etc.). Choose the reference you want, say, maltreat; go to entry 649.7 in the text section; under 649, it reads badness, and also refers you to see entry 648, which is its opposite, goodness. Under the decimal .7, you will find the words grouped according to their ideas rather than alphabetically like in other dictionaries. Search the word "abuse" in the Internet's version.

■ Examples of some of the subject or technical dictionaries are:

  Dictionary of the Environment. 3d ed. New York: New York University Press, 1989.

  Dorland's Illustrated Medical Dictionary. 29th ed. Philadelphia: Saunders, 2000.

  New Grove Dictionary of Music and Musicians. Washington, DC: Grove's Dictionaries, 1980. 20 vols.

To find dictionaries and other reference sources on the Internet on the topic of your choice, you might use Yahoo! <http://www.yahoo.com/Reference/>. Alternatively, search Web dictionaries at: <http://www.onelook.com/> or Alta Vista <http://www.altavista.com> by entering:

+science +reference
+art dictionar*

Encyclopedias defined

> **Encyclopedia** or **encyclopaedia** n. [Med. Lat. *encyclopaedia*, general education course.] A comprehensive reference work having articles on a broad range of subjects or on numerous aspects of a given field, usually arranged alphabetically (*Webster's II New Riverside University Dictionary*, 1984 p.430).

Encyclopedias are used to find: an overview article on people, historical events, ideas, topics ranging from arts, crafts, sports and hobbies to sciences and technology — a good place to begin your library research (see Figure 1.7 in Chapter 1). Encyclopedias also include reference sources and related material, subject headings, cross references, illustrations, maps, photographs, charts, as well as factual data.

■ Examples of types of questions suitable for encyclopedias are:

1. An overview article on Thomas Jefferson.
2. A report on tropical forests; those in the Ndoki region of central Africa are of special interest.
3. An overview article on Brazil.
4. The impact of acid rain in different countries in North America (US, Canada, Mexico).

EXERCISE 4.1: Looking up an encyclopedia article

Take any general printed or Web-based encyclopedia, e.g., *World Book Encyclopedia*, *Encarta* or *Encyclopedia Britannica*, printed or online <http://www.eb.com/>.

1. Try to find an article on Thomas Jefferson, the first question above.

2. Take note of the special types of features, such as pictures, photographs, maps, as well as a list of acronyms, biographical sketches, the bibliography at the end of the article, an index, and introductory notes.

Among the special features of the Web-based *Encyclopedia Britannica*, you will see different buttons: ARTICLES, INDEX, IMAGES, and TABLES. Click on the Index button first; read briefly about Jefferson's association with John Adams; also find his theories on education as well as on human rights. Read about the Declaration of Independence. Switch to other buttons, say the Articles button. You can always CLEAR your search and go to the next.

Main types of encyclopedias

The main types of encyclopedias are: general or comprehensive encyclopedias and subject or technical encyclopedias.

■ Example of a general or comprehensive encyclopedia is:
   The New Encyclopedia Britannica, 15th ed. Chicago: Encyclopedia Britannica, 1992, 32 vols. <Britannica online http://www.eb.com/>

■ Example of subject encyclopedia is:
   The New Palgrave: A Dictionary of Economics. New York: Stockton Press, 1998. 4 vols.

How to use encyclopedias While dictionaries typically organize their entries alphabetically, some encyclopedias group their entries by ideas rather than alphabetically; for that reason, many encyclopedias use indexes to provide an easy access to their articles. Rule of thumb: the larger an encyclopedia, the more likely it will group entries by topics. Typically, one-volume encyclopedias arrange their entries alphabetically.

Other factual sources

This section looks at representative factual sources aside from dictionaries and encyclopedias. These sources contain specific pieces of information and often provide compilations of factual and statistical data about places, nations, and /or persons. Examples of factual sources are almanacs, yearbooks, handbooks, directories, and various geographical sources including maps, atlases and gazetteers. You will soon learn specific titles in each of these classes of reference sources.

Factual sources, or factbooks, are used to find information about statistical data (almanacs, yearbooks); about people and organizations (handbooks, manuals, directories); and to locate geographical locations (maps, atlases, and gazetteers). Specifically, the types of questions that lead to factual sources are:

1. Addresses, phone numbers, web home pages of scientists, famous athletes, Nobel prize winners, entertainers, congressmen, schools, new books, libraries, educational programs for high school students in the U.S. by school district, and so on.
2. Cities in the Brown County (Indiana) (telephone areas).
3. Health district profiles for Los Angeles County requested by a headmaster who is building a recreational facility for his high school.

Almanacs, yearbooks, handbooks, and directories defined

Almanac n. [Med. Lat. *almanach*.] 1. An annual publication including calendars with weather forecasts, astronomical information, tide tables, and other related tabular information. 2. An annual publication of lists, charts, and tables of useful information.

Yearbook n. A documentary, memorial, or historical book published every year, containing data about the previous year.

Handbooks contain concise information with tables, graphs, formulas, symbols; these are often written in technical language. Other handbooks may be in the areas of literature, the arts, etc.

A **directory** is a list of persons, organizations, services, or chemicals.

■ Representative examples of factbooks are:

Almanacs:
Information Please Almanac. Boston: Houghton Mifflin Co., 1974 to date.
<http://www.infoplease.com/> Search on specific countries such as
El Salvador; what type of information does this Almanac provide?
Can you see a map of El Salvador? You may want to compare
this Almanac with the one that is written for kids:
<http://www.factmonster.com/>.
World Almanac and Book of Facts. New York: World Almanac, 1962– .
(Annually compiled information ranging from actors, energy, U.S. his-
tory and vital statistics).
For the Internet's version of the *Old Farmer's Almanac*, see
<http://www.almanac.com/>.
For worldwide coverage of countries, see *CIA World FactBook* at:
<http://www.odci.gov/cia/publications/factbook/>.

Yearbooks and handbooks:
Statesman's Year-Book. New York: St. Martin's Press, 1864- .
Consumer's Resource Handbook, 1992 ed. Washington DC: Office of
Consumer Affairs.
Handbook of Chemistry and Physics. Boca Raton, Fla: CRC Press.
Bartlett's Familiar Quotations. 16th ed. Boston: Little, Brown & Co.,
1992 <http://www.bartleby.com>.

■ Your directory guides in searching for colleges and career information:
Occupational Outlook Centers contains information for nearly 800
occupations in major areas with wages, demand, and education
requirements <http://stats.bls.gov/ocohome.htm>.
Peterson's Guides to Schools is now on the Web:
<http://www.petersons.com/>.
Princeton Review maintains its Web page with information about colleges,
tests, and more:
<http://www.review.com/>.
National Center for Education Statistics publishes surveys that are of special interest to teachers, librarians, and parents <http://nces.ed.gov/sur-
veys/>. Elementary/Secondary Surveys are on Private Schools, Crime
and Safety, on the Census School District 2000, and many others.
For information on Internet local sources, visit the Internet Public Library
Youth Division <http://www.ipl.org/youth/> and click on USA government. Learn about the three branches, the Constitution, and state governments. Another excellent source is Los Angeles Public Library's
Guide to the Web <http://www.lapl.org/inet/inet.html>. Select
"politics and government" and choose any state for local links.

Federal information is divided into general information that offers access to the U.S. Government Printing Office, Statistical Abstracts of the U.S., the National Archives and Record Administration, and other resources. The Executive Branch will link you to Immigration and Naturalization Service and the Social Security Administration. The Judicial Branch includes full texts from Supreme Court Cases, the Senate and the Congress. There are other links to the United Nations and Embassies. Don't forget to use your telephone directories, which pack useful sources and addresses of local offices.

Locating geographical sources

Geographical sources are maps, atlases, and gazetteers. We will begin to look at some of the representative titles of each of these sources.

A map is a representation on a flat surface of the whole earth or part of an area. While many maps are drawn on single sheets, they compile a lot of information, in fact multiple layers of information. For example, a single map might contain a base map, cultural, geophysical, and political characteristics of a given area. In addition, it may also show names of water bodies, streets, urban elements and other patterns covered by the area it portrays. We list the main types of maps:

1. Area maps and atlases (by scale, maps are of large, medium, or small scale).
2. Thematic maps and atlases may be general purpose maps representing physical and cultural features, as well as special purpose maps that differ by content/theme or subject (e.g., geological, natural resources, soil, environmental, economic, demographic, health).
3. Historical maps (e.g., History of the United States) often with illustrations.
4. Gazetteers, which are dictionaries of place names.

■ Examples of maps:
   U.S. Geological Survey. National Atlas of the United States. Washington: Government Printing Office, 1970. It contains more than 300 pages of maps and a 41,000-entry index. First part has "general reference maps" (1:200 million) plus urban area maps (1:500,000), and thematic maps.

■ For maps on the Internet, visit the following cites:
   <http://www.npac.syr.edu/textbook/kidsweb/SocialStudies/geography.html> includes an interactive Map Viewer, U.S. Gazetteer that allows you to search for the locations of towns in the United States, and maps of the world.

<http://tiger.census.gov> will give you the "Coast to Coast" digital map database; you can redraw your own maps for your neighborhood, your county, your state, etc.

<http://www.lib.utexas.edu/Libs/PCL/> and visit Map Collection; it will show you Perry-Castaneda Library Map Collection. Online maps of general interest are historical maps, maps of The Americas, of Europe, of the Middle East, of the World.

<http://www.lib.virginia.edu/exhibits/lewis_clark/home.html> displays maps from Columbus to Lewis and Clark explorations.

<http://www.mapquest.com> allows you to find the best route from your place to any other town in the continental United States.

■ Examples of atlases and gazetteers:

Chambers World Gazetteer. Cambridge: Cambridge University Press, 1990.

National Geographic Atlas of the World, 6th ed. Washington, D.C.: National Geographic Society, 1992.

Rand McNally New Cosmopolitan World Atlas, Census ed. Chicago: Rand McNally, 1991.

Historical Atlas of the United States. Washington, DC: National Geographic Society, 1988.

EXERCISE 4.2: Looking up maps

Visit a map collection in your library and locate maps of:

1. El Salvador, Nicaragua, and Mexico (any country).

2. For each country, locate major cities, bodies of water, and mountains.

3. How do you find things on a map? Does it provide a legend, an index, textual information, and any other explanations?

Evaluation of reference sources

(of particular interest to teachers, parents, and to anyone who wishes to buy reference books)

Once we have identified and located items of interest, especially through informal channels, remote catalogs, and bibliographies on the Web <http://www.amazon.com>, we need to evaluate these reference sources. For the coverage of reference sources, readers are referred to this chapter and Chapter 5. We list reviewing sources in this section because these are important titles for teachers, parents and anyone who wishes to buy a dictionary, almanac, encyclopedia, and other reference books. Librarians, however, are trained and experienced in the art of evaluating reference sources. We also assume that experienced teachers are well versed in matters of the selection process in general, and intellectual freedom, in particular. Other interesting and controversial topics include the meaning of collection development in a time of global information access where an e-book (electronic book) may be competing with a p-book (printed book) in the near future. For an introduction to e-books, visit <www.softbook.com> to sample Stephen King's "Riding the Bullet."

Well known bibliographic sources include *American Historical Fiction, Senior High School Catalog,* and *Subject Guide to Books for Intermediate Grades.* Other reviewing sources include: *Booklist, Horn Book, Journal of Youth Services in Libraries* (the Association for Library Service to Children, Young Adult Library Services Association), *Library Journal, School Library Journal, School Library Media Quarterly,* (Journal of the American Association of School Libraries). Yet other sources are prepared by educational organizations for social studies, humanities, sciences, the arts, and foreign languages.

The process of evaluation is an analytical one and requires guidance and practice. We have included points to consider which are important in evaluating *reference sources* such as encyclopedias and directories (Chapter 4). The same criteria apply to biographical sources (Chapter 5).

Evaluation of reference sources The purpose of reference sources, as defined earlier, is to rapidly locate a book, to show tables of statistical data and various distributions in a particular place and time, to give information about schools, people, services, and so on. These pieces of information are typically not related to one another as are individual chapters in a novel or a report. For example, words in a dictionary are arranged alphabetically rather than by their meaning. Therefore, reference sources are used differently from topical sources due to differences in their structure. Because the structure of reference sources is made up of files, entries, and data elements, people scan through selective entries only; they do not read entries sequentially and cover-to-cover. These characteristics of reference sources are important to keep in mind throughout the evaluation process.

One of the most important points to consider is the *preface*, often referred to as an introduction. It describes the organization of a work, its content, special features, and how to use it.

Next consider the author's name and the title page of a source. Both are applicable for printed and electronic sources regardless of their form (e.g., dictionary, directory, almanac, magazine title, as well as books and articles).

The *author* may be a person, a group of people, an editor, an agency, or a publisher. Some publishers, including government bodies, are well-established producers of various reference sources. Examples are the American Library Association, H. W. Wilson Company, Gale Research, and the United States Department of Education.

Special attention should be given to the *title page* of a source as it gives the fullest amount of information for the purposes of identification, citing, and evaluation. The title page may also contain the title and subtitle of the source as well as an edition statement. The publication date is equally important to consider. As a rule of thumb, use the most current edition of a work. Other elements that you will typically find on a title page are the name of the publisher and the place of publication.

What you have learned

Key points to remember about factual sources include:

1. The type of reference material factual sources are.
2. Appreciation of a variety of factual sources that exist in different media.
3. What sorts of questions are most suitable for encyclopedias, almanacs, and directories.
4. How to use the Internet to locate various factbooks.
5. How to evaluate reference sources taking into account their preface, author, and title page.

CHAPTER 5

Fact-Finding: People, Reviews, Criticism

In this chapter you will learn to:
1. Use different types of biographical sources in your library research
2. Make use of reviews and other factual material
3. Differentiate between reviews and literary criticism
4. Search library catalogs for book-length biographies

Almost every day you read about people in the news, ranging from President Bush, to people in entertainment, artists, athletes, ordinary people, and deceased people. Where do we find information about people?

In this chapter, you will also learn how to use reviews. People use reviews all the time as aids in selecting what to read, hear, and buy. Some people are just interested in what critics have to say about various literary and artistic productions. Before you go to a theater to listen to Tchaikovsky's opera, *The Queen of Spades*, you wish to read a bit about the composer, his work, and the society he lived in. You want to buy a book for your youngest brother. You want something that will answer those timeless questions such as how did the camel get its hump? The leopard his spots? And exactly, who invented words? Where do you turn to?

In addition, literary criticism can be a valuable reference source, especially when used to substantiate an opinion or perspective on a subject.

This chapter will introduce you to some basic biographical sources, reviews, and literary criticism.

Biographical sources

Biographical sources are used to verify the spelling of names, to find biographical data (biographical dictionaries, yearbooks, almanacs), and for general information about a person (encyclopedic biographical dictionaries).

For the moment, remember that there are many different types of biographical sources each of which is designed to answer specific questions. Don't worry about individual titles; we will cover those shortly. Choose a few people that you find intriguing (e.g., contemporary African American poetess Maya Angelou; Roger Sherman, 1721-1793; Abigail Adams, 1744-1818; Samuel Langhorne Clemens, known under Mark Twain; Ernest Hemingway). You will need at least one page for each of the persons. What are some of the questions you need to answer? HINT: is the person living? Is the person living in the U.S.? Consider the person's gender and profession.

Recall the roadmap (Figure 1.7 in Chapter 1) that illustrates the relative place of biographical sources compared to other reference books in your hypothetical search process. Typically, your search will start with encyclopedias and dictionaries. Each of these sources contains some information about people but does not go into great detail. An exception is the library catalog, which gives access to book-length biographies.

Characteristics of biographical sources

Biographical sources vary on the following five characteristics (Figure 5.1). Some include information about living people only, while others give information about both people living and deceased; some biographical sources are general and cover many different professions; others might include notable women and their contributions in science alone. Some have international slant

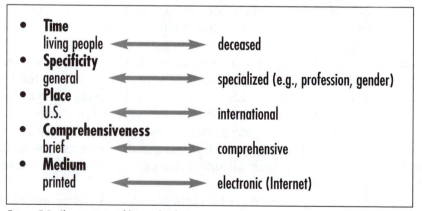

Figure 5.1: Characteristics of biographical sources

while others consider the Americans. Biographical sources might range from brief data about people to full-length chapters. Finally, some sources will be printed books; others may include multimedia together with interviews and excerpts from people's lives.

EXERCISE 5.1: Finding biographical sources

If you wish to read about Jerry Garcia (Grateful Dead), Sandra Bullock (American actress), or any other personality of your choice, which of these five characteristics would you use?

Jerry Garcia:

Sandra Bullock:

EXERCISE 5.2: Which source is the best source

Answer the following questions about the five people below by using library catalogs and/or encyclopedias only. For example, is Kate Chopin living in the United States? What did/does she do? Which source (encyclopedia title, library book) did you use to answer these questions?

PERSON'S NAME	TIME: living: Yes / No Not sure	PLACE: U.S.: Yes / No Not sure	PROFESSION: Writer, composer, Politician, teacher	SOURCE: title (year):page #
T. Jefferson				
Thomas Dylan				
Joan Didion				
Toni Morrison				
George Sand*				

*Find a book by Belinda Jack's biography of George Sand, a 19th century French novelist, befriended by Chopin, Liszt, Delacroix, Balzac, and Flaubert. Reviews appeared in the New York Times Book Review, and other papers. Read about her artistic developments and intellectual atmosphere in early 19th century France.

Organization of biographical sources

Biographical sources may be divided into two large groups: sources about **living people** and those about **deceased people**. Each of these two sources may be subdivided into the U.S. general and specialized sources and the world general and specialized sources. Below, we give examples for these types of biographical sources. In addition, there are some general Internet links that you might want to explore:

■ <http://lii.org/> then click on **People**; **Literature**, then on **Authors**; select **Art** and then click on **Artists**, etc.

■ <http://www.biography.com/>
What is Jimmy Carter's full name?
Your answer:

_____

■ <http://www.s9.com/biography/>
When was Pinochet the president of Chile?
Your answer:

_____

■ <http://www.ipl.org/ref/RR/static/ref1000.html> compiles numerous links to biographical sources under **Artists & Architects**; **Authors**; **Entertainers**; **Musicians & Composers**; **Politicians & Rulers**; **Scientists & Inventors**. This site includes biographical references in the following categories: African American History; American Women's History: A Research Guide; Distinguished Women of Past and Present; Spanish-language resources for biographies of famous people from all over the world including royalty and world leaders, writers, actors, musicians and singers, artists, athletes, the Nobel Channel, and more.

Living people

An example of a general printed biographical source for persons living in the U.S. is *Who's Who in America*. In addition, there are a variety of specialized *Who's Who* biographical sources (e.g., in American Politics; Aviation and Aerospace; Golf; Science and Technology). An example of a specialized biographical source is: *American Men & Women of Science: A biographical dictionary of today's leaders in physical, biological, and related sciences*, 20th ed. New Providence, N.J. : R. R. Bowker, 1998. Check the following Web sites for biographical information:

■ *The Cambridge Biographical Encyclopedia* with about 15,000 entries; it is on the Web at:
<http://www.biography.com/>
Find anything about Bill Cosby (his age, full name, birth place, profession, etc.)

- <http://www.s9.com/biography/> searches more than 25,000 notable men and women from ancient times to the present day.
  Search for information about your historical figure (e.g., Paul Revere, John Adams)
- <http://www.celebsites.com/> maintains links to TV and movie artists, athletes, writers, musicians.
  Find information about Whoopi Goldberg, Ben Affleck, or your favorite film, sport, and/or entertainment personality.

EXERCISE 5.3: Looking up brief biographical information

Find biographical information about Bill Clinton. What is Clinton's full name? Which law school did he attend? What sort of biographical detail is given? Which of the sources above would you use in order to answer these questions?
Your answers:

Deceased people

- U.S. general and specialized sources:
  Dictionary of American Biography. New York: Scribner, 1973–1994.
  Notable American Women, 1607-1950. A Biographical Dictionary. Cambridge, Mass.: Belknap Press of Harvard University Press, 1971, 3 vols., suppls.
  U.S. Congress. Biographical Directory of the American Congress, 1774–1996. Alexandria, VA: CQ Staff Directories, 1997.
- World general and specialized sources:
  Webster's New Biographical Dictionary. Springfield, Mass.: Merriam-Webster, 1988.
  Dictionary of Scientific Biography. New York: Scribner, 1970–1990, supplements.

General remarks If you are hunting for book-length biographies, search your library catalogs. Specifically, to get book-length biographies from your school library catalog, simply type in the person's name; if you are searching larger library catalogs, you may want to attach the following subheadings to the persons' names.

Examples:
NAME of the person you are researching, plus any of the following:

biography	in literature
correspondence	manuscripts
criticism and interpretation	technique
fiction	youth
interviews	style
quotations	

To get biographical information from magazine articles, search *ProQuest* and *NewBank*. You will find current information from newspaper articles: <http://www.latimes.com/>, <http://nytimes.com/>.

For information on less-known people around the world, check search engines, such as <http://www.altavista.com/> or <http://www.google.com>. For example, to search for Nicaraguan poets, simply type in their names: e.g. **"Ernesto Cardenal."** As a result, you will get Web pages that give you information about this Nicaraguan poet.

Why would you look for a (book) review?
Reviews are used for a variety of reasons. Consider the following examples:

1. To see what critics say about a book (to get critical evaluations or opinions on a work, style, character, and sometimes biographical data).
2. To understand what a book is about (to get a summary of the work, plot, key issues raised). Here, summaries are usually descriptive rather than evaluative.
3. To aid in selecting which works to read or which performances to see.
4. To get a quick reference for a work's characters, dates of premiers, and cast.
5. To obtain biographical information about the author.

The purpose of a review is to give people an accurate idea of a work, such as a film, book, play, dance performance, or exhibit, so that they may be more knowledgeable prior to seeing the film, or purchasing the book. A review is different from a critique. Reviews announce films, books, and plays; describe topics and methods, discuss technical qualities, actors, directors, and examine its merits compared to other similar works. Reviews usually appear shortly after the publication or the production. Many books are never reviewed. In contrast, a critique is far more evaluative than a review; the critic usually writes about works that already have some standing and assumes that the reader has already seen the work.

Some of the most important sources for book reviews are newspapers, such as *Los Angeles Times, New York Times, Washington Post*; magazines including *Time, Newsweek, Cosmopolitan*, academic journals, as well as review publications (*Science Books & Films, Choice, New York Review of Books, New York Times Book Review*). Many of these sources are on the Web: <http://lii.org/> Then choose Literature and Reviews.

The most widely used review sites are:
BookWire <http://www.bookwire.com/>
Booklist <http://www.ala.org/booklist/index.html>
New York Times Book Review <http://www.nytimes.com/books/>
The New York Review of Books <http://www.nybooks.com>
Audiobooks <http://www.idsonline.com/terraflora/audio/>

NOTE: Remember to cite sources for review articles in your reports.

EXERCISE 5.4: Source(s) for current book reviews

1. Where would you look for a current book (theater, movie, concert) review?

2. What is the difference between a book review and a critique? Please write your answers in the box below:

Literary criticism

The purpose of literary criticism is to evaluate literary works by novelists, screenwriters, poets, short story writers, playwrights, science fiction and non-fiction writers. Furthermore, it may involve studying the authors' lives, comparing and contrasting different writing styles, ideas, motifs, and symbolism used in a work, or applying theory to texts or movements in literature.

Some of the sources that may help start your search for information are encyclopedias and library catalogs. A more specialized source is the *Columbia Dictionary of Modern Literary and Cultural Criticism*. Another prominent reference book that defines and discusses terms, critical theories, and points of view that are commonly applied to the classification, analysis, interpretation, and history of works of literature is *A Glossary of Literary Terms*.

If you search library catalogs for books on literary criticism, you will find the following subject headings (LCSH) useful in your exploration:

American Literature—United States
American Literature—United States—20th Century
American Literature—United States—Women Authors
American Prose Literature—Colonial period, ca 1600-1775
American Prose Literature—History and Criticism
Children's Literature
Criticism—History
Criticism—History—20th Century
Literary criticism in the Renaissance

Figure 5.2: Search for books on literary criticism

In addition to some of the sources that were noted earlier in this chapter, here we list just a few more sources for literary criticism:

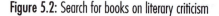 *Contemporary Literary Criticism. Excerpts from criticism of the works of today's novelists, poets, playwrights, short story writers, scriptwriters, and other creative writers.* Detroit: Gale Research, 1973- .

■ Magill, Frank N. *Masterplots*, rev.ed. Englewood Cliffs, NJ: Salem Press, 1976, 12 vols. *Survey of Contemporary Literatur*e, rev. ed., 1976, 12 vols.

The Contemporary Literary Criticism (CLC) series includes critical commentaries on more than 2,000 authors now living or who died after December 31, 1959. Each *CLC* volume contains about 500 individual excerpts taken from numerous book review periodicals, general magazines, scholarly journals, and books. Entries provide critical evaluations spanning from the beginning of an author's career to the most current commentary. Entries also include portraits when available, principal works, explanatory notes, and whenever possible, previously unpublished interviews. Further readings appear at the end of entries on authors for whom a significant amount of criticism exists in addition to the pieces reprinted in *CLC*.

Specific writers and their literary work are well represented on the Internet. For example, for an overview of Shakespeare's plays, resources, and online editions of his works, check the Web's first edition of the *Complete Works of William Shakespeare* at <http://www-tech.mit.edu/Shakespeare/works.html>.

What you have learned

Key points to remember about the various biographical, review, and literary criticism sources include:

1. What sort of reference material biographical sources are, and how they are represented in library catalogs and periodical literature.
2. Understanding the major differences that exist between reviews and literary criticism.
3. What sort of questions are most suitable for biographical sources, for reviews, and for literary criticism material.
4. How to use library catalogs to find out which length-size biographical sources are available.
5. How to use online services, such as *ProQuest*, as well as on the Web, to locate various reviews and biographical sources.

CHAPTER 6

Finding Books, Maps, Reference Sources

In this chapter you will learn:
1. To search library catalogs for books, maps, and other reference sources
2. To interpret data in library catalog entries
3. To apply different search strategies for different information needs
4. To evaluate topical sources for artistic and literary excellence

This chapter will introduce you to the effective uses of library catalogs in general. You will search books and reference materials in your local library catalog. In addition, you will learn about remote and larger library catalogs on the Internet. The Chapter closes with a discussion on how to evaluate information for their artistic and literary excellence.

What are library catalogs?
Library catalogs are reference sources that provide bibliographic entries to documents, such as books (NOT parts of books), and maps. For example, Figure 6.1 (see next page) gives enough information to help you decide if the book, *Sport in Greece and Rome*, would be potentially relevant to you. By "enough information" we mean information contained in the data elements, including authors' names, title, publication data, physical description of the book, and subject headings. So instead of going to the library stacks and browsing books there, you first search the catalog which will save you time and more efficiently show you the books that you need. In effect, the library catalog is to libraries what an index and table of contents are to books. Use of the catalog allows you to find and browse books.

It is important to understand that catalogs give access to book-like materials and not to, for example, magazine articles. It is also useful to know what kinds of information needs are well suited for library catalogs. The following are representative types of questions that may be addressed by library catalogs:

- Are there any illustrated collections of myths from around the world?
- Did Benjamin Franklin write any autobiographical books?
- What is the correct spelling of Angelou's name?
- Are there any books on rock music in Southern California?
- Are there any books on education in ancient Greece and Rome?
- Does the library have encyclopedias on Latin American history and culture?

Author:	Harris, Harold Arthur.
Title:	Sport in Greece and Rome / H. A. Harris.
Published:	Ithaca, N. Y. : Cornell University Press, c1972.
Description:	288 p. : illus, ; 23 cm.
Series:	Aspects of Greek and Roman life.
Subject(s):	Sports—Greece.
	Sports—Rome.

Figure 6.1: Cataloging entry for a book

EXERCISE 6.1: Looking up by topic

Your librarian will show you how to use the library catalog for finding publications on various TOPICS. Search the library catalog and give answers to the following questions:

1. How many books did you find on **solar energy**?

2. Circle different class numbers that are given to books on solar energy:

   [5xx]   [6xx]   [3xx]   [other] write down class number

   REMINDER: go to Chapter 2 to see Dewey Decimal Classification (DDC) for detailed subdivisions. Alternatively, see Appendix A, or visit <http://www.ipl.org/youth/dewey/>.

3. Look at the subject headings that are assigned to the books on solar energy; are there any new subject headings that you may use to find more books on solar energy or a similar topic? Write down subject heading(s) other than **solar energy** that are given to books on solar energy:

   subject heading 1:

   subject heading 2:

   subject heading 3:

   Go to the library and locate a book on your topic, e.g., **solar energy**. If the book is not there, look around the missing book and locate a book on the same or similar topic.

   OPTIONAL: Cite the book in the space below using the format for books in Chapter 9.

EXERCISE 6.2: Looking up for people

Your librarian will explain how to search the library catalog for PEOPLE.
Find books on **Samuel Adams**—you need information for a research report on *how Samuel Adams influenced the development and growth of early American politics, government and society*. You will probably receive from your history teacher a list of other important figures from early American history.

Search for books about **Samuel Adams**.

1. How many items (books) did you find?

2. Which class numbers are they given?

   REMINDER: see Chapter 2, or click on <http://www.ipl.org/youth/dewey/> to get a description of the 10 Dewey Decimal classes.

3. Now look at several entries on your screen; what subject heading(s) are assigned to these books?

   subject heading 1:

   subject heading 2:

   subject heading 3:

4. Use these subject headings to find more books on Samuel Adams or similar topics. Go to the library shelves and locate a book on your topic. If the book is not there, look around the missing book and locate a book on the same or similar topic.

   OPTIONAL: Cite the book in the space provided below using the format for books in Chapter 9.

EXERCISE 6.3: Looking up places

Your librarian will show you how to search for PLACES. Search your local catalog for books on **Mexico**.

1. How many books did you find that are related to Mexico?

   Notice that books will cover various aspects: Mexican culture, revolutions, the art of ancient Mexico, Pre-Columbian civilizations (e.g., Aztecs and Mayas), cookery, travel, maps, literature, geography of Baja California (Mexico), customs, immigration.

2. How many books did you find in class 3xx (social sciences)?

3. Note the subject headings of the books grouped in the 3xx class; write down several subject headings:

   subject heading 1:

   subject heading 2:

4. How many books are in 6xx class (technology, applied sciences)?

5. Search the library catalog under the heading: Art, Mexican. Are there any illustrated books in English? If so, list two titles and the corresponding call numbers below:

   Title 1:   Call number:

   Title 2:   Call number:

EXERCISE 6.4: Identifying individual data fields in a cataloging entry

Look under mythology. If your library does not have this particular book on mythology, use the catalog entry in Figure 6.2.
Locate a book by Virginia Hamilton and answer the following questions:

1. Write down its full title including the subtitle:

   Title:

   Subtitle (part of title that follows the ":" symbol:

2. Is this book illustrated?　　❑ Yes　　　　　❑ No

3. What is the call number of this book?

EXERCISE 6.5: Using library catalogs to find books, not magazine articles

1. Can you find journal articles in library catalogs? For example, can you find in your **library catalog** an **article** titled "Coral eden," by David Doubilet that appeared in the National Geographic magazine, volume 195, number 1, January 1999?　　❑ Yes　❑ No

2. Can you locate the book below in your library catalog?　　❑ Yes　❑ No

Author:	Fowler, William M., 1944-.
Title:	Samuel Adams: radical puritan
Published:	New York : Longman, c1997. xii, 190 p.: ill.: 20 cm.
Series:	Library of American biography
Subjects:	Adams, Samuel, 1722-1803.
	United States. Declaration of Independence—Signers—Biography.
	Puritan—United States—Biography.
	United States—History—Revolution, 1775-1783.
Call number: 973.3 FOW	

Figure 6.2: Cataloging entry of a book in a series

3. Can you locate an encyclopedia article on the 2000 Democratic National Convention (August 2000 in Los Angeles) in a library catalog?　　❑ Yes　❑ No

---

Main objectives of library catalogs

Library catalogs are designed:

1. To show what the library has when you know the author's name, the title, or both. Examples: Mark Twain's *Huckleberry Finn*. William Fowler's *Samuel Adams: radical puritan.*
2. To show what the library offers on a given topic. Examples: United States Declaration of Independence; solar energy; mythology.
3. To show all books by (and about) an author. Examples: Mark Twain; Maya Angelou.
4. To show what the library offers in a particular form of literature, such as encyclopedias, fiction, cartoons. Examples: encyclopedias of Latin America.

In the first case, you will typically *know* some of the following information: the author, the author and some title words, and perhaps a precise title. The earlier example, *Samuel Adams: radical puritan*, is an example of a "known-item search" where the author/title is known.

In the second case, you might know the topic or *subject* — what the book is about, hence "subject search" (United States History Revolution, 1775-1783). To search library catalogs by subject, libraries use *subject authority files*. An example of such a file is the Library of Congress Subject Headings (LCSH), discussed in Chapter 2. The purpose is to bring together all variants under one subject heading so that the material about the same or similar subjects can be brought together in one place. Consequently, documents which are represented with synonymous terms to mean the same thing — lawyers, attorneys, council— can be looked under one subject heading in the catalog rather than scattered alphabetically under the three headings.

The third feature is unique to library catalogs. Maya Angelou's works might be found under M. Angelou, Maya Angelou, or some other variation. Library catalogs establish and maintain one name for each author, so that you can find everything that he or she has published under that one name. The example in Figure 6.3 shows a typical case of a well-known American writer, Samuel Langhorne Clemens, who wrote under his more popular name, Mark Twain. So, even if you did not know Twain's real name, you would retrieve all his publications from the library catalog.

Clemens, Samuel Langhorne, 1835–1910
SEARCH: Twain, Mark, 1835–1910

Figure 6.3: Name Authority File

The fourth feature of library catalogs assists in locating the precise type of literature on a desired topic. Examples include dictionaries and encyclopedias, interpretation and criticism, and fiction.

EXERCISE 6.6: Learning to search library catalogs with different access points

Try to locate the publication below in your library:

> **Author:** Walser, Robert.
> **Title:** Running with the devil : power, gender, and madness in heavy metal music / by Robert Walser.
> **Published:** Hanover, NH : University Press of New England, 1993.
> **Description:** xviii, 222 p. ; ill. ; 24 cm.
> **Series:** Music/culture
> **Subject:** Heavy metal (Music)—History and criticism.

1. How would you search the above book in your library catalog by author?

2. How would you search the above book in your library catalog by title?

3. How would you search for books on the same/similar topic in your library catalog?

4. Using the Dewey Decimal Classification (see Chapter 2), where would you find this book in the library? Mark only one box of the four possibilities below:

❑ class 500 (science/metals)   ❑ class 700 (arts/music)
❑ class 600 (applied science)   ❑ class 300 (social studies/culture)

Beyond your local library catalog

In order to search beyond your local library for the topics in Exercises 6.1 to 6.7, visit the following Internet resources:

- To search for books worldwide, enter:
  <http://www.bookwire.com/index/libraries.html>
- To explore archival collections, enter:
  <http://sunsite.berkeley.edu/FindingAids/>
- To browse children's literature page, enter:
  <http://www.scils.rutgers.edu/special/kay/childlit.html>

Putting library objectives into practice:
Examples from Melvyl®

This section is of particular importance to juniors and seniors as they prepare for college. Teachers and media specialists may also be interested in searching large union online catalogs of numerous academic and research libraries. One such example for the state of California is Melvyl®, a service of the California Digital Library <http://www.cdlib.org/>.

What is in Melvyl®? It provides access to all major library collections of the state of California. It holds more than 27,000,000 records from the OCLC® Online Union Catalog for books, computer files, audiovisual materials, periodicals, maps, manuscripts, and musical scores in a variety of languages. The database does not include individual articles from journals, newspapers, or book chapters. **Searching Melvyl®** <http://www.melvyl.ucop.edu> is possible for known items and subjects, as discussed earlier.

Evaluation of topical sources

Topical sources differ from reference sources with regard to their *structure*. For example, topical publications are divided into interrelated chapters, rather than files, entries, and data elements (see a section on evaluation of reference sources in Chapter 4). The structure is influenced by the main intent of most topical sources: to tell a story in a certain way, to develop characters in a story, to evoke a particular mood or scenery; to introduce certain phenomena, describe experiments, and to draw conclusions. A reader responds to this accordingly: it is natural to read a novel in a linear fashion, from one chapter to the next starting with Chapter 1, in the order written by its author.

Here are the reasons why evaluation is important:

First, not everything that you have managed to retrieve will be equally valuable to your interest, or reliable in content. Of the potentially relevant items, you need to sift through the information based on authority, artistic and literary excellence. Second, there might be a wealth of information that you cannot use directly in your work; for example, the material is too expensive to obtain, or it is outdated or difficult to understand.

The process of evaluation, also known as critical thinking, is an analytical one and requires guidance and practice. Topical publications are obtained from library catalogs, bibliographies, such as <www.barnesandnoble.com> or <www.amazon.com>, magazine databases, and sometimes, the Internet. Specifically, topical publications include books that you have obtained through the library catalog search. Other topical publications may be magazine and newspaper articles, reviews, short stories, and individual chapters of books that you have obtained through the database search. All of these sources have one feature in common: they are read for either information or enjoyment. Once we have identified and located items of potential interest, we need to evaluate these topical sources.

Evaluation of sources

One of the most important points to consider is the author's name and the title page of a source. Both are applicable for printed and electronic sources regardless of their format (e.g., books, maps, albums and articles). Many authors nowadays will have their personal Web pages with links to their credentials, affiliations, and their work. In order to find out about the author, simply type in the author's name in the Google search engine <www.google.com>, or read Chapter 5 for biographical sources.

The *author* may be a person, a group of people, an editor, an agency, or a publisher. He or she may also be a creator of artistic work (a painter, choreographer, music director, music writer, sculptor, and photographer). Examine the credentials and affiliations of the author and creators. Some publishers, including government bodies, are well-established producers of various topical and reference sources. Examples are the American Library Association, National Geographic Society, and the United States Department of Education.

Special attention should be given to the *title* page of a source as it gives the fullest amount of information for the purposes of identification, citing, and evaluation. The title page of books may also contain the title and subtitle of the source as well as an edition statement. The publication date is equally important to consider. As mentioned in Chapter 4, other elements that you will typically find on a title page are the name of the publisher and the place of publication. The title page of articles will have information about volume, issue, pagination, and the title of the entire journal (*Ceramics, Newsweek, Science*).

Analogously to the preface in most reference books, there is an introductory section in most topical books and articles. It gives a motivation statement, main objectives, and questions that will be addressed in the main body of the article. Presence and the overall quality of bibliography should always be examined for scope, accuracy, and currency. Other features are as important; these are presence and quality of illustrative and supportive material, index, and data collection instruments.

What you have learned

Chapter 6 focuses on searching online library catalogs in general. The following themes are discussed:

1. What library catalogs are and what they contain.
2. What sort of information you would need to have in order to use catalogs effectively.
3. What information is included in a library catalog entry.
4. What topical sources are and how to evaluate them.

This chapter has introduced the following concepts. We review only the most important terminology:

Collocation　　　　Grouping together documents by a recognizable attribute, such as grouping books by their topic, value, author, and size.

Corporate author　　A party responsible for intellectual or artistic content of works; examples are governmental agencies, associations, schools, and churches.

Melvyl®　　　　　An online library catalog, produced by the University of California Office of the President; it provides access to nine UC library holdings, California State libraries and many other academic and special collections in the state of California.

Name Authority File　A list of established forms of names (personal, corporate, series), which must be used in searching library items.

Online Catalog　　　A library catalog that is searchable online.

Series   A group of separate items related to one another by the fact that each item bears, in addition to its proper title, a collective title applying to the group as a whole. In the earlier example, "Running with the devil," there are many books that belong to the same general series titled Music/culture.

CHAPTER 7

Searching & Evaluating Internet Sources

In this chapter you will learn how:
1. To search Web sources that you use in your work
2. To locate basic sources that are related to your classes as well as health, education, and life-long information needs such as finding a college
3. To evaluate information sources on the Internet

The Internet has been defined as the international network of networks. Here, we view the Internet as a worldwide digital collection of useful resources that will help you explore and research. For example, it provides access to college directories <http://www.petersons.com/>, <http://www.collegegrad.com/>, <http://www.review.com/>, collections of textual and graphical data (e.g., <http://www.ditto.com>) as well as access to shopping <http://www.amazon.com>, and the latest information on sports <http://espn.go.com>. The Internet has become a unique global community forum for debate, exploration, learning, entertainment, and self-development. But can it bring global peace, cut pollution, eradicate cancer and other diseases through the human genome project, and reduce inequality? For answers to some of these questions, read an article, "What the Internet cannot do," in Economist <www.economist.com/> August 19th, 2000.

This view of the Internet makes an important distinction between the Internet as an information resource and the Internet as a communication service. This chapter focuses on conceptual aspects of the Internet as a collection of information resources. Accordingly, Chapter 7 will focus on search engines and respective search strategies. We will use examples that will be relevant in your classes and outside of school activities. Exercises will give you hands-on experience in searching and evaluating networked resources.

In particular, the Think Guide for Chapter 7 reviews criteria for evaluation of Web documents; it is located in back of this Chapter. In addition, Appendix B provides a copy of the Acceptable Use Agreement for users of the Internet.

Introduction to the Internet: A brief look

The Internet is both a vast collection of information and a communication system of computer networks worldwide. All these different networks communicate with each other using the same telecommunication protocol, Transmission Control Protocol/Internet Protocol (TCP/IP). Locally, you are connected to a host computer that directly provides services regardless of the operating system of your computer or workstation. The host computer is linked through regional networks to the national backbone of networks.

Internet tools, such as the World Wide Web or the Web, allow you to access and find interlinked hypertext-based multimedia documents. There are various browsers which help you navigate and search the Internet's vast resources. Examples of Internet browsers include Netscape and Microsoft Explorer. To search the Web, people use various search engines, robots, and meta-search engines:

- Yahoo! at <http://www.yahoo.com>
- AskJeeves at <http://www.askjeeves.com>
- Google at <http://www.google.com>
- Meta-search engines such as <http://www.searchenginewatch.com/>
- Dogpile at <http://www.dogpile.com/>

For a detailed comparison of 10 different search engines, see Think Guide for Chapter 7 in back of this Chapter.

Each Netscape page <http://home.netscape.com/> gives the following features:

1. Highlighted words and images in the content area of the page which, when pointed at, open new Internet pages on the screen.
2. Toolbar buttons activate commonly used Netscape features, such as Back, Forward, Home, Reload, Images, Open, Print, Find, and Stop.
3. Directory buttons link to pages with information and tools for browsing, such as "What's New!," "What's Cool!," "Handbook," "Net Search," and "Net Directory."
4. Pull-down menu items activate features similar to toolbar buttons.
5. Location field above the content area shows the location of the current page.
6. Progress bar fills with color as a transfer operation completes.

There are two main modes of searching the Internet's resources. For an *exploratory* search, use hyper-text links that will take you to related Web documents. For a more *direct* search, you need to know the address of the Web document or the Uniform Resource Locator (URL); enter it directly into the URL location area and search for specific keywords. As an example for the exploratory search, link to a subject guide directory Yahoo! <http://www.yahoo.com> and choose any of the broad subject classes from the main menu. These are subdivided into more specific subject categories, which in turn contain lists of Web documents on various topics, events, and other resources.

Every Web document is assigned a standardized unique address called a URL, as noted above. The address specifies the method of access (http:// for HyperText Transmission Protocol), the address of the host (www), the computer on which the data or service is located (sjsu), and the type of domain (*edu* for education; *gov* for government; *com* for company; *org* for organization), sometimes a path/or names of files (.depts/Beethoven/). So, the entire URL for the sources about Ludwig van Beethoven is: <http://www.sjsu.edu/depts/Beethoven/>. All Web documents use the HyperText Markup Language (HTML) for creating hypermedia documents. Web documents are typically written in HTML language and are designated with the suffix ".html". There are numerous Web tutorials and authoring sources. Here is one of many such sources:<http://www.cwru.edu/help/introHTML/toc.html>.

EXERCISE 7.1: Finding Web documents by browsing

Browse and discover: If you are still in Yahoo!, click on one of the main categories. What subdivisions do you see on your screen? Explore other subdivisions, such as <u>Fitness</u> and <u>Sports</u>.

1. Can you find a list of genetically engineered foods?

   Write down the entire series of categories from the broadest to the most specific one. Describe your search in the space below:

2. Go back to the main menu. You are looking for historical information. Which of the main categories will most likely give you information about the U.S.– Mexican War (1846-1848)? Use the space below for your search description. Write down the entire sequence of choices that you made before you got your sites on the U.S.– Mexican War.

EXERCISE 7.2: Finding Web documents by knowing URLs

URL-known search: If you know the URL address of an electronic resource on the Web, enter the location. From there, point-and-click on any among the subject headings to see specific Web sites. You can save your Web sites with the Bookmark feature (pull down the bookmark menu, and click on add). Some sites are of special importance to parents <http://www.ala.org/parents/index.html>, <http://www.tekmom.com/>, teachers <http://ericir.syr.edu/>, and media specialists <http://www.ala.org/ICONN/index.html> as well as <http://www.windwardlibrary.net>).

How to think critically about Web documents

Since not all Web documents are equally well suited and valuable, this section introduces you to four types of criteria to evaluate material produced on the Web. These criteria are: authority, content, structure, and search features. Under each of these 4 headings, we suggest questions to help you evaluate Web documents.

Authority

1. Is the producer/author of the Web page given? Is there a distinction made between the author of the content, the Webmaster, and the contact person? (for your information, the author is typically a person or an organization responsible for the intellectual and/or artistic content of the Web page; the Webmaster is typically a programmer who is responsible for coding content into the HTML language).

2. If the author, editor, or creator of the intellectual content of the Web page is given, are links included to their credentials and affiliations? This is important because it gives you an opportunity to get in touch with the author in order to obtain more detailed information, explanation, and further clarification on various issues.

3. Which sector is represented in the domain part of the address (edu—for education, gov—for government, com—for company, org—for organization)? Typically, university and governmental sites are free of charge, tend to be of higher quality, and less biased than the commercial sites. Check also some excellent -org Web sites; these are produced by non-profit organizations such as the Public Broadcasting Service, PBS <http://www.pbs.org/>, the Internet Public Library <http://www.ipl.org/> and other sites put out and maintained by professional organizations such as the American Mathematical Society <http://www.ams.org/> and numerous sites that are put out by the American Library Association for kids, schools, parents, and teachers <http://www.ala.org/ICONN/>.

Content

1. What does the Web page contain?
2. Is the Web page designed for advertising/promotional purposes?
3. Does the Web page offer "further readings," bibliographies, and other useful links?
4. Can you detect any bias (gender, political, ethnic, racial)?
5. Is the use of graphics (images, icons, animation) relevant to the content? Would you be equally satisfied if you searched the text-only version?
6. Is the date and update frequency given?
7. Are appropriate credits given to the sources used in the document?
8. Is the site designed for a specific audience in mind, such as middle school students, high school students, parents, teachers, administration, researchers, or for everybody?

Structure

1. Comment on the general structure, hot links, and the use of other navigational tools.
2. Have you detected any error messages, blind links, "under construction" sites, or outdated URLs?
3. Is the layout on the screen well designed (well labeled? easy to read?)?
4. Is the page designed in a layered mode? (or just about everything is put on the main page?)

Search features

1. Are there "help" screens and online tutorials with examples available?
2. Which search modes exist currently? (simple search, advanced search)
3. Does the engine support easy search modification?
4. Are navigational tools self-explanatory?

The following section contains useful Web pages from a wide variety of sources and on different topics. Now that you know how to evaluate Web material, check the pages below in terms of the four types of criteria that we have just introduced: Authority, Content, Structure, and Search Features.

1. **URLs of governmental information sources:**

    <http://thomas.loc.gov/>
    A collection of full text legislation and major bills.

    <http://www.loc.gov/>
    The official Web page of the Library of Congress containing documents that describe the library and its history, exhibits and events, digital library collections, and more.

<http://lcweb2.loc.gov/amhome.html>
The American Memory Project at the Library of Congress consists of primary sources and archival materials relating to American culture and history. Most of these offerings are from the Library's special collections.

<http://tiger.census.gov/>
Online maps of the United States sponsored by the U.S. Bureau of the Census; use its browser to redraw maps with various features such as county lines, highways, parks, water bodies, cities, streets, and census tracks; other features include zoom-in and zoom-out controls.

<http://www.census.gov/>
U.S. Bureau of the Census publishes authoritative summary of mainly federally collected statistical data. It is supplemented by Historical Statistics of the U.S., Colonial Times to 1970.

<http://www.census.gov/statab/www/>
Statistical Abstract of the U.S. including data on population, employment by occupation, personal income, consumer price index, sales by kind of business, U.S. exports and imports.

<http://www.usgs.gov/>
U.S. Geological Survey features science topics including those on global warming and protection of coral reefs.

<http://www.odci.gov/cia/publications/factbook/country.html>
CIA World FactBook gives detailed information about worldwide countries.

Other Web documents related to *health* and *health statistics* include:

<http://www.cdc.gov> (Centers for Disease Control and Prevention)
This CDC home page is also available in Spanish. The Page contains *Emerging Infectious Disease Journal* (EID Journal) that tracks trends and analyzes new and reemerging infectious disease issues around the world. You can read information from *Morbidity and Mortality Weekly Report* (MMWR). Of special interest is "Travelers' Health", how to protect yourself from disease when traveling outside the U.S.

<http://www.who.int/> (World Health Organization, WHO)
This Web page is also available in multiple languages. You can access WHO reports and other documentation about communicable diseases, disease outbreak news, statistical data, and various health topics.

<http://www.osha.gov/> (Occupational Safety and Health Administration, OSHA)
Read about OSHA's proposed new ergonomic standard and its new 'Plain Language' workplace poster.

<http://www.ncbi.nlm.nih.gov/PubMed/>
PubMed is a project developed by the National Center for Biotechnology Information, NCBI, at the National Library of Medicine. PubMed gives you access to bibliographic information in the fields of medicine, nursing, dentistry, veterinary medicine, and the health care.

<http://igm.nlm.nih.gov/>
Internet Grateful Med, produced by the National Library of Medicine, offers access to a wide variety of health-related databases, including PRE-MEDLINE, AIDSLINE, AIDSDRUGS. A special feature is the ability to find specialized search terms from NLM's Unified Medical Language System.

Important Web resources related to presidential debates and *political parties* are:

<http://www.democrats.org/> The official Web site of the Democratic National Committee highlights its platform, online polls, debates, campaign trail, and other news from the headquarters.

<http://www.rnc.org/> The Republican National Committee homepage offers information on RNC's history, issues, and proposals. You might be interested to read the 1912 Platform of the Progressive Party, also known as "Bull Moose Party" <http://www.ssa.gov/history/trplatform.html>. The Party opposed the conservatism of the regular Republican Party and called for aggressive social legislation. For more information about the Reform Party, click on <http://www.reformparty.org/.>

2. **URLs of education-related sources** (of special interest to teachers, librarians, parents):

- Classroom CONNECT <http://www.classroom.net/> offers information for educators, students, parents, and anyone interested in teaching, learning, and information technology.

- The AskERIC virtual library <http://ericir.syr.edu/> offers collections of numerous Web sites including: education Listservs Archives; Newton's Apple lesson plans for use with the PBS Science Series; and Discovery Communications programs. Search ERIC Digests, produced by 16 ERIC Clearinghouses, at: <http://ericir.syr.edu/Eric/>.

- Visit the Flinton Public Library list of resources for Web sites, books, articles and videos on civics in general, culture, education, and active citizenry: <http://www.flint.lib.mi.us/fpl/resources/civic/civic.html>

- Examine the following education-related URLs keeping in mind the four evaluation criteria:

  <http://sunsite.berkeley.edu/KidsClick!/> The site searches more than 600 topics, such as facts and people, mythology, society and government, literature, sports and recreation, geography and history; click on machines and transportation and visit an annotated list of sources on robots and robotics.

  <http://www.ipl.org/teen/> Find out how Internet Public Library (IPL) selects material (in "teen division policy"). The site contains information ranging from homework to career and college, health, math and science, sports, as well as politics and government.

- Teachers and media specialists will find the following Web resources useful for their class preparation and special projects:

  <http://www.ala.org/ICONN/index.html> This site is an initiative of the American Association of School Librarians (AASL). Excellent sources are organized for students and the entire family.

  <http://www.ed.gov/> This is the U.S. Department of Education home page. It gives access to ERIC Digests, technology, National Library of Education, finding K-12 schools and colleges; it lists contacts, funding opportunities, and more.

  <http://goldmine.cde.ca.gov> California Department of Education has organized its home page under the following main headings: Teaching, Learning & Technology; State & School Finance, Research & Statistical Information; Healthy Children, Youth & Families; Special, Alternative & Continuing Education; Legal & Legislative Information; and Funding Opportunities.

- For science programs, go to Mad Scientist Network <http://www.4kids.com/kidscnc.html>. In addition, for curriculum resources, visit SCORE Science lessons for high school grade levels: <http://scorescience.humboldt.k12.ca.us/>. You can search for lesson plans that have a clear connection to science standards, that are problem-based, and are specific to your subject matter and grade level. For example, by selecting grade level 10 and genetics, we retrieved excellent lesson

plans, also known as WebQuests. "DNA for dinner?"
<http://www.gis.net/~peacewp/webquest.htm> by W. E. Peace, for example, is well linked to curricular standard that is specific to the 10th grade; the lesson is divided into sections: Introduction, Task, Process, Resources, Evaluation, and Conclusion.

- For math Web programs, visit Swarthmore Dr. Math
  <http://www.forum.swarthmore.edu/> as well as Cornell Gateway
  <http://www.tc.cornell.edu/MathSciGateway/math.html>.
  Also check instructional resources at the SCORE history site:
  <http://score.kings.k12.ca.us/>.

- For Social Studies lessons, visit SCORE History site:
  <http://score.rims.k12.ca.us/> and then search for specific grade levels
  and topics. My search for 10th grade (World History and Geography: The
  Modern World) gave numerous lesson plans, each containing resources
  and activities.

EXERCISE 7.3: Fill-in data from Web documents

To see a collection of some of the best images from NASA's planetary exploration program, enter:
<http://pds.jpl.nasa.gov/planets/>

Enter EARTH; fill-in the following data:

Average distance from the Sun: _____

Highest point on the surface: _____

Rotation period (in Earth hours): _____

Revolution period (length of year): _____

Internet as a worldwide digital collection

We will navigate and search hypertext-based resources on the World Wide Web, or Web, by means of using search engines, such as Alta Vista, Infoseek, and Lycos; subject guides, such as Yahoo!, and meta-search engines such as Metacrawler. Here, we introduce only the representative search engines and meta-search engines. See Think Guide for Chapter 7 in back of this Chapter for comparison between 10 Internet search tools.

Search engines

Alta Vista <http://www.altavista.com/> relies on robot-generated tools to collect and index Web resources. It provides access to millions of Web pages. To get started, point to the SIMPLE button at the top of the page and then select HELP for an online tutorial on simple queries. Advanced queries use operators such as AND, OR, NEAR, and NOT. It also allows for ranked matches so that those pages with the highest scores are placed at the head of the retrieved list.

Searching with Alta Vista As we have just mentioned, there are two levels of searching with the Alta Vista search engine: simple search and advanced search. To give you some hands-on experience in searching these two modes, we will run a search first in the simple mode and then repeat the same search in the advanced mode.

The search is as follows:

A Christmas Carol by Charles Dickens (both author and title are known)

Simple search
Search 1: A Christmas Carol by Charles Dickens. Type in Dickens' Christmas Carol. How many hits did you get?

Now type in "Dickens Christmas Carol." How many matches did you get now?

Advanced search and analysis of the results
The search title: Dickens' NEAR "Christmas Carol" resulted in five relevant items. Compare the results of this search to the simple search that yielded 200,000 items. Knowing how to use specific search features pays off.

InfoSeek <http://guide.infoseek.com/> searches Web pages, Usenet news, several news wire services, computer periodicals, and movie reviews. To search effectively, it is useful to consult its online Guide for search features.

Lycos <http://www.lycos.com/> searches Web pages, File Transfer Protocol (FTP), and gopher sources; it offers long entries (extracted from the URL, header fields, frequently used words) and short entries (extracted from the URL and up to 16 lines of hyperlink text from other pages). Lycos uses Boolean operators, proximity operators, and rank documents.

Webcrawler <http://webcrawler.com/> is a "Web robot" which searches full texts of Web pages, FTP, and gopher resources. Search features include the AND and OR operators, relevance weighting, and the ability to discover documents.

EXERCISE 7.4: Comparative searches using different search engines

In order to get a feel for different search engines, as well as to compare the search process and results, run the following search topics across several search engines, including Yahoo! <http://www.yahoo.com/>, Alta Vista <http://www.altavista.com/>, and Dogpile <http://www.dogpile.com/>.

1. Benjamin Franklin (write your search here; also give the URL):

Hunt for bonus points:
2. Map of early American colonies; explain how you got it and give URL below:

3. Lewis and Clark expedition (a map); explain how you found it and give the URL below:

4. Declaration of Independence — illustrations and text; explain how you got it and give the URL here:

Subject directories and meta-search engines

Yahoo! <http://www.yahoo.com/> is a searchable and browsable hierarchical subject directory; every site added to Yahoo! is examined by a human cataloger. The simple search looks for the keywords in categories, titles, and comments, and returns the first 100 matches. The advanced search uses Alta Vista as the search engine.

Each site is assigned a subject category as well as subcategories. For example, the main page shows the following broad categories (Fig.7.1)

Art and Humanities
(literature, photography...)

News and Media
(TV, papers)

Business and Economy
(finance, jobs...)

Recreation and Sports
(sports, travel, outdoors)

Computers and Internet
(games, software...)

Reference
(libraries, quotations)

Education
(K-12, colleges & universities)

Regional
(countries, US)

Entertainment
(cool links, movies, humor, music)

Science
(astronomy, engineering)

Government
(elections, law, taxes)

Social Science
(archaeology, economy, languages)

Health
(medicine, fitness)

Society and Culture
(people, religion)

Figure 7.1: Yahoo!'s main subject categories

EXERCISE 7.5: Learning to use Yahoo's hierarchies

Using Yahoo!'s main page <http://www.yahoo.com/> with the broad categories, find information on El Salvador's schools, travel, and government. Select the Yahoo! en espanol button if you wish to read Yahoo!'s sites in Spanish.

HINT: click on **Regional**. Notice the new URL in the box. Find the **country** of your choice (Nicaragua, El Salvador). Now click on **education** to find information about their schools, contacts, etc. Again, there is a new URL address. If you want to go one level back (to the education subcategory), click on the Back button; for two-levels back, press the Back button twice.

Metacrawler <http://www.metacrawler.com/> is a multi-threaded Web search service that was originally developed at the University of Washington. Use the main menu to search the Web. Alternatively, click on any of the hyper-links to read sports scores and news, and to check other topics for your reports. The left hand-side bar offers additional table of contents, including information about MetaCrawler (MC) history, Frequently Asked Questions (FAQs), MetaSpy, and Power Search features.

In summary, the following page is a listing of representative Internet finding tools.

Name	Young adult	Meta-search engine	Search engine
Alta Vista http://www.altavista.com			Simple, advanced mode, Operators: + and; - not
Ask Jeeves www.askjeeves.com			Simply type in your question: natural language query
Ask Jeeves for kids http://www.ajkids.com	7-12th grade students		Human selected sites for 7-12th grade students (as opposed to robot-selected sites).
Dogpile http://www.dogpile.com	Kids like it	Searches several search engines (known as multi-threaded searches)	
Excite http://www.excite.com Google http://www.google.com			Simple, advanced mode, Operators: and, or, not Fast, precise, simple search engine (****)
Lycos http://www.lycos.com			No boolean operators, fast, easy, simple
Searchenginewatch www.searchenginewatch.com		Excellent multi-threaded engine (****)	
Yahoo! http://www.yahoo.com			Subject directory for the general public
Yahooligans! www.yahooligans.com	Subject directory for kids (****)		

Figure 7.2: Internet finding tools

What you have learned

Chapter 7 presents an overview of searching digital libraries focusing on conceptual aspects of searching. This Chapter particularly emphasizes a hands-on approach to searching the Internet's search engines.

Equally important is the section on *How to think critically about Web documents*. We list URLs of a wide variety of information sources in different disciplines and then suggest that you explore some of these and evaluate them in terms of evaluation criteria. A separate section compares and discusses simple and advanced search techniques. The searches are done across the most popular search engines and meta-search engines. The following list includes selective terms and some of the concepts that have been introduced in this chapter.

HyperText Markup Language (HTML) A subset of standardized general markup languages **Language (HTML)** used to create Web documents.

Internet The collective name for a worldwide network of computer networks using the same telecommunication protocol (TCP/IP for transmission control protocol/ Internet protocol) distributed net.

Microsoft Explorer® A browser used to access Web documents.

Multimedia An integrated information consisting of text, photographic images, animation, sound files, and video clips in digital form that creates a stand-alone or networked product.

Netscape Navigator® A browser used to access Web documents.

URL Uniform Resource Locator that allows a standardized form of addressing the location of Web documents on the Internet.

World Wide Web A graphic hypertext-based system for finding and **(WWW)** accessing Web resources via hot links and buttons.

Think Guide for Chapter 7: Evaluation of Web Sources

How to think critically about Web documents

Since not all Web documents are equally well suited and valuable, this section introduces you to four types of criteria that you could use to evaluate the material produced on the Web. These criteria are: authority, content, structure, and search features. Under each of these 4 headings, we suggest questions that will help you to evaluate Web documents.

Authority

1. Is the producer/author of the Web page given? Is there a distinction made between the author of the content, the Webmaster, and the contact person? (for your information, the author is typically a person or an organization responsible for the intellectual and/or artistic content of the Web page; the Webmaster is typically a programmer who is responsible for coding the content into the HTML language).

2. If the author, editor, or creator of the intellectual content of the Web page is given, are links included to their credentials and affiliations? This is important because it gives you an opportunity to get in touch with the author in order to obtain more detailed information, explanation, and further clarification on various issues.

3. Which sector is represented in the domain part of the address (e.g., edu—for education, gov—for government, com—for company, org—for organization)? Typically, university and governmental sites are free of charge, tend to be of higher quality, and less biased than the commercial sites. Also check some excellent -org Web sites; these are produced by non-profit organizations such as the Public Broadcasting Service, PBS <http://www.pbs.org/>, the Internet Public Library <http://www.ipl.org/> and other sites put out and maintained by professional organizations such as the American Mathematical Society <http://www.ams.org/> and numerous sites that are put out by the American Library Association for kids, schools, parents, and teachers <http://www.ala.org/ICONN/>.

Content

1. What does the Web page contain?
2. Is the Web page designed for advertising/promotional purposes? Does the Web page offer "further readings," bibliographies, and other useful links?
3. Can you detect any bias (gender, political, ethnic, racial)?
4. Is the use of graphics (e.g., images, icons, animation) relevant to the content? Would you be equally satisfied if you searched the text-only model?

5. Is the date and update frequency given?
6. Are appropriate credits given to the sources used in the document?

Structure

1. Comment on the general structure, hot links, and the use of other navigational tools.
2. Have you detected any error messages, blind links, "under construction" sites, or outdated URLs?
3. Is the layout on the screen well designed (e.g., well labeled? easy to read?)

Search features

1. Are there "help" screens and online tutorials with examples available?
2. Which search modes exist currently? (e.g., simple search, advanced search)
3. Does the engine support easy search modification?

CHAPTER 8

Finding Magazine and Newspaper Articles

In this chapter you will learn to:
1. Find articles in magazines, newspapers, and journals
2. Distinguish primary from secondary sources in your research
3. Distinguish popular magazines from scholarly journals
4. Use different search strategies for different information needs

This chapter will introduce you to the various ways of finding information in periodical literature such as magazines and newspaper articles. The term periodical means any publication that is issued continually. The frequency varies; some periodicals, like dailies, come out each day, such as the *Washington Post* <http://www.washingtonpost.com/kidspost>, and the *Los Angeles Times*; some are issued weekly, such as *Newsweek*; others are published monthly, four times a year, and so forth. Instead of scanning through issues of hundreds of individual magazines, newspapers, and journals, many people typically use magazine databases, also known as periodical indexes. Just as library catalogs give you access to books, online magazine databases provide access to individual articles in magazines and newspapers. These databases are designed to save you time and to make your library research easy and effective. Examples of online magazine and newspaper databases are *ProQuest* <http://proquest.umi.com>, *NewsBank* <http://infoweb.newsbank.com/> and *SirS* <http://www.sirs.com>. Increasingly, online databases offer full-length articles. All three services are password protected.

Introduction to online databases

Online databases such as *ProQuest* are secondary bibliographic sources which provide access to primary sources (e.g., articles in magazines, newspapers, journals) by title, subject, author, and often other access points. This database, like many others, provides access to both scholarly and popular magazine articles.

Scholarly articles are peer-reviewed by experts in a given field for validity, originality, completeness, and bibliographic honesty. The articles are signed, bibliographies are extensive, and articles appear in journals that are published by academic and scientific societies. Examples are the *American Scientist, Nature, Scientific American*, and the *Journal of Applied Physics*. On the other hand, **popular magazines** feature extensive advertisements of commercial products and services, articles of popular content typically written by journalists and staff writers. The articles are current and often not signed.

NOTE: Online databases, such as *ProQuest*, *NewsBank*, and *SirS*, do not show the location of items in individual libraries. In our example, "Panic over power," you would either find the article in the July 17 issue (1989) in your local library, or request the article electronically through your e-mail account. Alternatively, your librarian can borrow an item from another library through a service known as an inter-library loan.

The following are just examples of topics that are suitable for periodical literature:

- Any articles that discuss the safety record of current Piper Saratoga single engine non-commercial planes.
- Any stories on the first democrats. A friend has mentioned to you an article that appeared in *U.S. News & World Report*. She thought that the article was published in the summer of 2000.
- Research on attitudes toward injury risks. Specifically, you are interested in the use of helmets in the prevention of motorcycle accidents.
- Any current newspaper articles about Nicaraguan poetry (written by ordinary people).

Of special importance to librarians and teachers is Appendix H in back of this book; it contains a checklist for contacts and summaries on these three online database services.

Your library may be subscribing to several online databases such as *ProQuest, NewsBank* or *SirS*. They are comparable and certain search features apply to all. For example, many articles are available in full length. They are password protected. The contents are searchable by means of using a simple search and more advanced techniques. They use "Boolean operators" that we have introduced you in Chapter 3. Your librarian and/or teachers will select the best database for your particular curriculum.

Examples of searching from ProQuest

Now we want to show you how to effectively search *ProQuest* <http://pro-quest.umi.com>. Your library may have already bookmarked *ProQuest* for you so you can use it to connect directly next time. It gives comprehensive access to magazine articles. There are several ways to search *ProQuest*:

1. **Searching by Word** using the **basic** and the **advanced** techniques.
2. **Searching for publication** that allows you to look for specific issues of a magazine.
3. **Searching by topic** that lets you select articles from broad topics.

■ The easiest way to familiarize yourself with the *ProQuest* online database is to select the "searching by topic" option. You can enter a topic in a dialog box or browse any of the 11 broad topics from the following main menu:

Critical issues	Plants & animals
Earth science	Social studies
Health	Sports & entertainment
In the news	Teacher topics
Industry & technology	The arts
People	

If you are looking for articles on **acid rain**, you might start off by exploring the "critical issues" topic. It is subdivided into more specific topics, such as assisted suicide, capital punishment, environment, gun control, immigration, animal rights, and political freedom. Since acid rain affects our **environment**, you will probably select this subtopic, which in turn, will show you even further subdivisions: access to articles about **acid rain**, the greenhouse effect, pollution, and rainforests. Each of these specific topics will contain about 50 articles that you can selectively print or e-mail to your account.

EXERCISE 8.1: Topical search

Using the Topic Search option, find information on acid rain that destroys Virginia streams. Cite one of the articles you found in the space below (see Chapter 9 on how to cite):

Using your browser's BACK button, go to the main menu and explore other topics. Alternatively, you may want to click on the NEW SEARCH arrow in the upper left corner to initiate a new search.

EXERCISE 8.2: Selecting the closest heading

Suppose you decide to switch your interest to finding articles about the American Revolution. Which general topic would you choose? Look at the 11 topics on the previous page. How many "clicks" do you have to make before you find articles on your topic, American Revolution?

■ Another way to search *ProQuest* is to do a **search on publications**. It requires little or no typing of search terms; all you have to do is to click on list publications to view an alphabetical listing of hundreds of magazine titles, journals and newspapers that are included in *ProQuest*. If you know the particular title of a magazine, you can type in its title in the appropriate search box (adolescence; addictive behaviors; oxford).

ProQuest gives several options so that you can specify your search by time (current articles or from back files); by type of articles (from newspapers, magazines, reference books); and by search source (from citations and abstracts to full texts).

EXERCISE 8.3: Publication search

1. Click on <u>list publications</u> and visit *America's Civil War*. What is the latest issue of this magazine (volume, issue and date)?

2. Now select the September issue (vol. 12, issue 4, 1999) and find an article by Roy Morris, Jr. What is the title of this article?

3. What does the image show for the article?

4. Go back to the magazine titles and select *Civil War History*. Read about primary sources on women nurses in the *Civil War* (vol. 45, issue 2, 1999). Who wrote these stories?

■ Using **Search by Word-Basic**, find articles on energy. Click on the Subject list link to view narrower subjects of the term "energy." Write down these more specific terms:

_____

_____

Notice the different ways you can modify your search. Use some of these pull-down menus to search back files (1990-2000), or to restrict your search to full text articles only.

EXERCISE 8.4: Using time qualifiers in searching

Find the most current newspaper articles that discuss **energy conservation**. Use some of the limit features that we have just discussed. Write down your search plan in the space below:

- The **Search by Word-Advanced** option lets you run more sophisticated searches than the basic option. For example, if you wished to find articles about **Pete Sampras** (or any other person, place, event or topic), simply type in his name in a designated dialog box and qualify your search by selecting the "personal name" qualifier from the pull-down menu. This will make *ProQuest* hunt for articles that have been indexed with **pete sampras** in the personal name field.

   Take this opportunity to look at other qualifiers in the same pull-down menu; for example, you can ask to see a specific image of Cordoba (Spain) if your search is qualified by the "image caption." Other ways to limit your search are: abstract, title, author, geographic name, company or organization, image caption, and subject. This feature will make your search precise and effective.

EXERCISE 8.5: Geographic name qualifiers in searching

Using the advanced option, search for articles about **Islam** in **Spain**. Qualify the word **spain** to the "geographic name" field and use the AND operator between these two terms.

1. How many articles did you get that match your request?

2. Which among the first 10 articles contain text and graphics?

Bonus Questions:

3. How many articles are there on the **American Civil War** that contain illustrations?

4. Could you find anything that contains illustrations about **Christmas** during the **American Civil War**?

5. Write a bibliographic citation. (Hint: read Chapter 9 in this book or click on the Help, Help Contents, and How to Cite an Article <http://www.umi.com/k12/main/>.

EXERCISE 8.6: Multiple choice questions related to access

Where would you search for the titles below?

(a)

Author:	Fowler, William M., 1944- .
Title:	Samuel Adams: radical puritan.
Published:	New York : Longman, c1997.
Description:	xii, 190p. : ill.; 20 cm.
Series:	Library of American biography
Subjects:	Samuel Adams, 1722-1803. United States–History–Revolution, 1775-1783. United States. Declaration of Independence– Signers–Biography.

library catalog ❑   online magazine database ❑

(b)

Author:	Hamlin, Suzanne.
Title:	Researchers find cravings hard to resist. (Living Arts Pages). New York Times v144 (Wed, Feb 22, 1995):B1(N), C1(L), col 5.
Description:	illustration, other, 41 col in.
Subject(s):	Compulsive eating–Research. Food habits–Physiological aspects.

library catalog ❑   online magazine database ❑

(c)

Harry Potter and the goblet of fire, by J. K. Rowling. Illustrations by Mary Grandpre. First American edition, July 2000. New York : Scholastic Press.

library catalog ❑   online magazine database ❑

Consider the following topics and start off by KEYWORD searching:

■ Topics in social studies that are suitable for online magazine databases are: affirmative action; gun control; capital punishment; civil rights; immigration; contributions of, for example, Albert Einstein, Yo-Yo Ma, Monica Seles, Michael Jordan, Magic Johnson, Tiger Woods, Vladimir Nabokov to the American culture.

■ Topics in science that are suitable for online magazine databases are: regulation of air, water, soil and oil pollution; the greenhouse effect; acid rain in specific countries; renewable resources.

Indexes to collections of poems, short stories, and songs
Access to parts of books, such as chapters, individual short stories, poems, and plays are cited below.

■ Sears, Minnie E. *Song Index*. [n. p.] Shoe String Press, 1966.
■ Hazen, Edith P. *The Columbia Granger's Index to Poetry*. 10th rev. ed. New York: Columbia University Press, 1994.
■ *Short Story Index*. New York: H. W. Wilson, 1953- . Annual.
■ *Play Index*. New York: H. W. Wilson, 1952- . Irregular.

Indexes to historical newspapers online
Teachers, media specialists, and students who are interested in studying 19th and 20th century history, will find *Historical Newspaper Online* a fascinating and indispensable research tool. You can access Chadwyck-Healey *Historical Newspapers* through the **California Digital Library** <http://www.cdlib.org/>. As the Introduction says, "You will find the full text of articles illustrating British attitudes towards the United States in the early 1800s and then find references to articles dealing with American reactions to British events in the 20th century. You can trace the development of technology from the power loom to the space shuttle or the end of slavery and the enfranchisement of women." *Historical Newspapers Online* <http://historynews.chadwyck.com/> provides access to primary sources through the *Palmer's Index to The Times, 1790–1905* with *Palmer's Full Text Online, 17851870, The Official Index to The Times, 1906–1980*, and *Historical Index to The New York Times, 1851–1922*.

What you have learned

Some of the key points to remember about online magazine databases, or periodical indexes include:

■ What sort of reference sources online magazine databases, or periodical indexes are.
■ What sorts of questions are most suitable for online magazine databases.
■ Main approaches in searching online magazine databases (examples from *ProQuest*).

This chapter has introduced the following terms and concepts:

Abstract   Summary of an article.

Online database   Bibliographic source that provides access to online
                        articles in journals, magazines and newspapers.

Periodical   A publication in any medium issued in successive
                        parts bearing numeric or chronological designations
                        and intended to be continued indefinitely (e.g.,
                        newspapers, yearbooks, magazines).

Citing in Style and Summarizing

In this chapter you will learn how:
1. To cite sources regardless of format (text, picture) or medium (print, Web) in order to give credit to others' writings or ideas
2. To summarize a work

Understanding how to cite and summarize sources is both critical and basic to all types of research activities. In this chapter you will learn how to give credit to the sources used in your reports so that readers can examine the evidence presented. To do that we will be using *bibliographic citations*. We define a bibliographic citation as a record in precise and consistent form that gives details about an item used in your work.

Chapter 9 will also teach you how to summarize sources that you use in your writing. To *summarize* means to critically analyze sources with regard to their content and presentation. Finally, we will review new terms at the end of this chapter.

Why is citing important?

First, it gives you the evidence to say what you have said in your writing. Second, it helps the reader find an item used in your paper. If you must select a writing among several choices, cite the one which is published (rather than unpublished), peer-reviewed, such as a journal article rather than a newspaper article, and written or created by a well-known author/artist or institution rather than by a kindergarten-level student. Failure to give credit to the works and ideas of others' is called *plagiarism*. *Webster's II New Riverside*

University Dictionary (1984) defines plagiarism as follows: "**1**. To steal and use (the ideas or writing of another) as one's own. **2**. To take passages or ideas from and use them as one's own." (p. 898).

Whether you use a book, a sound recording, or any other source of information in your report, you need to give credit to these sources. Information and ideas that you obtain from electronic mail, discussion lists, and Internet sites should also be cited. The following example is a citation of the **book** by Benjamin Franklin, titled *Autobiography and other writings*. The book was published in New York by Penguin Books in 1986.

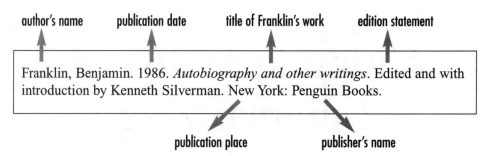

A typical bibliographic citation of a **journal article** consists of similar data elements: (a) the authors' name(s); (b) the publication date; (c) the complete title of the article; (d) the title of the journal in which the article appeared; (e) the volume, issue, and pagination. We cite these two items by using a set of rules given by one of the bibliographic style manuals, described shortly.

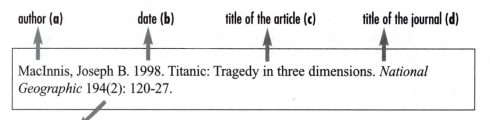

Typically, all *sources* used in reports may be classified as those which are communicated **formally** (books, journal papers, and maps) or **informally** (face-to-face communication and messages obtained via fax, phone, or e-mail).

Sources may also be of archival, primary and secondary nature.

Archival sources, such as personal papers and cultural heritage objects, are often used in novels and other writings; some of these sources are located at the Library of Congress: <http://lcweb2.loc.gov/amhome.html> and in other historical documents, such as, <http://earlyamerica.com/review/winter96/slavery.html>.

Primary sources, such as creative and technical writings, pieces of visual art and music, often draw on information contained in archival sources. All primary sources must be original in content, methods, ideas, and general techniques they use in their writings and works. In other words, an example of a primary source is the intellectual content of a book that did not exist before you wrote and published it. Another example may be an engineering invention that is protected and patented as an original design, system, or a program. Many other examples are in the areas of science, literature, art, music, and film making.

Secondary sources, such as catalogs and bibliographies, allow you to rapidly locate primary and archival sources of information. Examples of secondary sources are library catalogs (your school library catalog, and remote library catalogs, such as Harvard's at <http://hollis.harvard.edu/> and Getty's at <http://opac.pub.getty.edu>; bibliographies (*Books in Print*), and online magazine databases (*SirS, NewBank, ProQuest*).

The best sources for citing are:
1. the item itself (e.g., title page of a book, or an entire item like a map or a videotape with its container)
2. a library catalog for finding books, pamphlets, and atlases
3. the bibliography of an item you have used.

The sources just outlined give the most complete and accurate information for citing. To save time, whenever you use a source, make a complete and accurate citation of that source. This means that while you have an item, write down information about that item fully and accurately. If the item is a book, use information from both sides of the title page; copy the call number, the library which has the book (your school library, public library), and the way you searched and located the item in the library. Write down this information on large reference cards, or enter it directly into your computer files. Use the other side of the reference card for writing a brief summary of the item you used in your work. See Appendices I and J for templates on citing and annotating a book or an article.

Bibliographic style manuals
There are several widely used bibliographic style manuals that can assist you in properly citing the works that you have used in your writing. The following is a partial list of these manuals.

■ Gibaldi, J. 1988. *MLA handbook for writers of research papers*. 3rd ed. New York: Modern Language Association <http://www.columbia.edu/cu/cup/cgos/>.
■ *Publication Manual of the American Psychological Association*. 1994. 4th ed. Washington, DC: The Association. <http://www.apa.org/books/4200040.html> both in English and in Spanish.

■ Turabian, Kate. L. 1996. *A Manual for Writers of Term Papers, Theses, and Dissertations*. 6th ed. Revised by John Grossman and Alice Bennett. Chicago: University of Chicago Press.

How do you decide which style manual to use in your report? This is a matter of tradition, taste, departmental and personal preferences in your school and your teachers. It is important to remember that there are no bad styles. However, whichever bibliographic style you use for your bibliographies, follow its rules consistently and rigorously. For the purposes of introducing you to citing and making bibliographies, we will use *Turabian Manual* (1996).

As we move out of the Gutenberg era and into the electronic age more work is being produced and published in machine-readable form that may never appear in the traditional print media. While the *Manual* is fine for citing conventional material, it does not address "cybercitations" in great detail — how to cite the wealth of information available on the Internet. My students ask me how to cite various types of electronic sources in their papers. In response, this chapter includes templates for citing information that is available via millions of Web pages.

There are commercial citation software management programs for different bibliographic formats. Below, we have given a brief description of a widely used program.

■ EndNote Plus 2 (Niles & Associates) is a reference database manager that specializes in storing, managing, and searching for bibliographic references in your private reference library. It is also a bibliography maker—it automatically builds lists of cited works from word processing documents for in-text citations to compile a bibliography in many formats, including those cited earlier.

The following sections will show you how to cite different types of topical sources using the *Manual* (Turabian, 1996). We will take you through a series of seven cases; each case deals with a particular type of source that you may wish to cite in your writing (e.g., a book, an article; a Web site). While you can go directly to these individual cases and corresponding templates, we suggest that you follow the rules from the *Manual*; first, it is not possible to account for all possible cases that you might encounter in your reading and citing; second, the process of citing becomes less mechanical. However, we have attempted to capture the most representative cases that you will run into at the beginning of your report preparation. Each of the seven cases is described in the following four parts:

■ **Part 1:** *Find Pattern*. In this part, you will be given information that is typically found in items themselves; for example, if you have a book, you will find data elements including the name of the author, title, edition statement, publication place, publisher's name, and publication date. Together, these data elements, referred to as bibliographic information, are essential in citing. Data elements may be scattered on both sides of the title page and not necessarily in that order. Now that you know which typical data elements make up a bibliographic citation, your goal is to find various bibliographic patterns.

- **Part 2:** *Give Answers.* You will be asked to answer a set of questions related to the information that is given in the source.
- **Part 3:** *Find Rules* (**this part is optional**). With a bibliographic style manual in hand (Turabian, 1996), you will need to find rules that correspond to your answers in Part 2. Start with the Contents and the Index in the *Manual.* You may need to use several chapters and several rules to answer the questions posed in Part 2 in order to cite a source.
- **Part 4:** *Apply Rules to Patterns and Cite.* Finally, you will provide a citation as the "answer." You may find that some patterns do not easily match rules. In these cases, apply the closest rules. More importantly, think of the main purposes of citing, as discussed earlier.

Case 1—Question #1: how to cite a book

- **Part 1:** As shown in Figure 9.1, a title page of the book you want to cite has the following information:

Thomas Hutchinson and the
origins of the American Revolution

Andrew S. Walmsley

New York University Press

New York

Additional information is given on the back of the title page:

Copyright © 1999 printed in the United States of America

Figure 9.1: Title page of the book

- **Part 2:** To cite the above book, you need to answer the following questions:
1. How many authors are listed on the title page of this book?
2. What is the title of the book?

3. How about some publication data?
    (a) publication place:
    (b) publisher's name:
    (c) date of publication:

- **Part 3:** As mentioned earlier, for the purposes of this exercise, we will use Turabian's *Manual* (1996). We will use the reference list (RL) style (the Author-Date system, chapter 10) rather than bibliography (B) style (the Author-Title system, chapter 9).
- **Part 4:** If you are using the *Manual*, apply rules in order to cite the book. If you are not using the *Manual*, follow the template below in order to cite your own books that are written by a single author:

Template:

> Author's Last Name, First Name (Middle Name Initial, if given). Publication date. *Title of the book.* Publication Place : Publisher's Name.

Your answer:

> Walmsley, Andrew S. 1999. *Thomas Hutchinson and the origins of the American Revolution.* New York : New York University Press.

Case 2—Question #2: how to cite an encyclopedia article (printed version)

Template:

> *Title of the Encyclopedia*, edition., s.v. (means that you looked under word) "name of the person or place or topic that you looked under."

Your answer:

> *World Book Encyclopedia*, 15th ed., s.v. "Hutchinson, Thomas."

Case 3—Question #3: how to cite an encyclopedia article (Web version)

Template:

> "Title of the article," *Title of the Encyclopedia online*; accessed<date that you looked up>; available from < URL address >

Your answer:

> "Adams Family," *Encyclopedia Britannica online*; accessed <October 20, 2000>; available from <http://www.eb.gov:180/>

Case 4—Question #4: how to cite a story in a collected work

- **Part 1:** In this second example (see Figure 9.2), you will cite an individual story which is part of a collected work. "Europe" by Henry James is one of fifty-seven stories in *American Short Stories*. The title page has the following information:

> American Short Stories
>
> Fifth Edition
>
> Eugene Current-Garcia and Bert Hitchcock, both from Auburn University
> © 1990 HarperCollins Publishers

Figure 9.2: Title page from an anthology of short stories

- **Part 2:** Again, we need to answer several questions:
  1. Who selected these 57 stories?
  2. Is the publication place given?
  3. When was the 5th edition published?
- **Part 3:** Use rule 8.116 (for *short poems*).
  For question 2, use rule 8.52 (for *place of publication*); in particular, see rule 8.55 for cases where place of publication is not given; the abbreviation *n. p.* (for *no place*) is sufficient.
- **Part 4:** Follow the rules from the *Manual*, or use the following template to create your own bibliographic entries:

Template:

> Author's Last Name, First Name (Middle Name Initial, if given). Publication date of the entire book. "Title of the part you used." In *Title of the entire book*, ed. First Name, Last Name of the editor(s) who edited the entire book, pages. Place of publication : Publisher's Name.

Your answer:

> James, Henry. 1990. "Europe." In *American short stories*, eds. Eugene Current-Garcia and Bert Hitchcock. 5th ed. n.p. : HarperCollins.

Case 5—Question #5: how to cite an article

■ **Part 1:** In your paper you might have borrowed some ideas from an article published in the *Atlantic Monthly* August 1999, vol. 284, 19 through 21. The author and title are as follows:

> Can coffee drinkers save the rain forest? by Jennifer Bingham Hull

■ **Part 2:** As we did in the previous two examples, we need to answer some questions before we can cite the above article. Answers to the following questions will determine which rules you will use.

1. What is the type of publication? Circle one only:

    book   newspaper article   magazine article

2. How many authors have contributed to this writing?
3. Where does the writing appear?
4. Note all other data (publication year, volume number, pagination).

■ **Part 3:** If you are using the *Manual*, try to find the most appropriate rules. One of the most important decisions is to establish that the paper is an *article in a journal*, which leads you to rule 11.39. Note that different rules apply to magazine and newspaper articles.

■ **Part 4:** Here is a template that you can use to cite journal articles:

> Last Name, First Name (Middle Initial, if given). Publication date. Title of the article. *Title of the Magazine* volume number (Month issued) : pages of your article.

If you replace the above data elements, the answer will be as follows:

> Bingham Hull, Jennifer. 1999. Can coffee drinkers save the rain forest. *Atlantic Monthly* 284 (August): 19–21.

Case 6—Footnotes, endnotes

Some of your teachers may recommend the use of footnotes or endnotes. A rule of thumb for footnotes and endnotes is as follows: each time you cite a publication in your paper you should do the following two things:

1. In the paper: Identify your cited reference with a raised Arabic number half a space above the line. Example:

    > In a recent article on the air we inhale, we read that "although Los Angeles has the most polluted skies in the nation, it is one of the few cities where air quality has improved in recent decades."[1]

2. Cite the source either at the foot of the page (FOOTNOTE) below a short line, or at the end of the paper (ENDNOTE). Example for the footnote:

    ---

    [1]James M. Lents and William J. Kelly, Cleaning the air in Los Angeles, *Scientific American* 269 (1993): 32-39.

Case 7—Cybercitation templates

General guidance for citing material on the Internet is outlined in the following template (per rule 8.141 in Turabian, 1996):

> Author's Last Name, First Name. "Title of Work," accessed <date>; available from <URL address>.

If you replace the above parts with the corresponding data from a Web page, your citations are as follows:

> Vandergrift, Kay E. "Vandergrift's children's literature page," accessed May 15, 1999; available from <http://www.scils.rutgers.edu/special/kay/childlit.html>.

To see more examples on citing sources obtained through the Internet, see "A brief citation guide for Internet sources in history and the humanities," by Melvin Page. The address is: <http://library.byu.edu/~rdh/eurodocs/cite.html>. *A Guide to Citing Electronic Information* by Li and Crane is: <http://www.apa.org/books/pubman.html>. Learning Page of the Library of Congress contains guidelines for citing electronic sources: <http://memory.loc.gov/ammem/ndlpedu/cite.html>. In addition, see Appendix I for reproducible templates on how to cite basic formats.

How to write summaries?

This last part of the Chapter shows you how to summarize (annotate) sources used in your research. To summarize means to briefly state main points of an item that you used in your own writing. In order to avoid plagiarism, and teachers are good at recognizing this, it is important for you to know how to paraphrase the book or any other publication using your own words. See Appendix J which contains reproducible templates on summaries.

Tips:
1. An easy way to go about doing this is to divide the work into various sections relating to special features of the work, its organization, and so on.
2. You may first summarize a given work informally without using full sentences.
3. You can color code different parts of the text by importance, amount of information, and order you intend to use in your report.
4. Another technique is to graphically make clusters with similar information grouped in each separate cluster. For example, one cluster might include everything that is said about a character; a separate cluster could contain his or her relations with other people and events; another about his or her contributions to political ideas, and so forth.
5. An important part of writing a summary is understanding each word that you use in your own writing; having a dictionary or your textbook besides you might help you summarize efficiently and accurately.
6. Asking questions will make your report stronger, more interesting, and insightful.

We present two examples: how to annotate a book, and another example for an article. Each source is first cited; then we introduce temporary headings as prompts to remind you of important points to consider in annotating your sources.

NOTE: There are four basic rules to remember whenever you annotate documents used in your reports:

- Use your own words and not the authors' words.
- Mention highlights only rather than everything that is discussed in the document you are annotating. Separate important things from less important ones; be selective.
- Be critical of others' writings in a positive way.
- Include your own insight and understanding.
- Make connections.

How to summarize (annotate) a book: an example

U. S. Department of Health and Human Services. 1993. *Healthy People 2000 Review*. Hyattsville, Md: Government Printing Office. Annual.

Summary: A detailed account of data on health care expenditures and revenues, facilities, services, manpower, and health status of the U.S. population, 1970s to 1990 with trends from 1950 and some projections. Among special *features*, the book includes maps, prevention profiles, 143 detailed tables, appendices, description of data sources, definitions of terms and codes, and a subject index to tables. All are easily readable and understandable. In regard to *bias*, the publication provides adverse effects of smoking. It does not cover the right to smoke and other issues. The information is well *organized*, with general topics covered first, followed by definitions and evaluation of data sources.

Accuracy/currency: Data are gathered from federal government reports, surveys, databases, international and professional associations. The information is current. The information is intended for anyone interested in the health hazards of smoking. The publication packs much statistical and other factual data.

How to summarize (annotate) an article: an example

Raymer, Steve. 1993. St. Petersburg, Capital of the Tsars. *National Geographic* 184 (6): 96-121.

Summary: St. Petersburg (also known as Petrograd, or City of Peter as well as Leningrad) is a monument to the worldly aspirations of its namesake rule and his imperial successors, and has survived the communist years to rival Moscow as Russia's cultural center. The article also shows historical and city maps of St. Petersburg. In terms of *organization*, the article is typical of other magazine stories. It traces the city's rich and turbulent history since its birth in 1703, Russia's triumph over Napoleon in 1812, and the 1917 revolution. Special *features* are photographs of lavish mosaics gracing the Church of the Resurrection, ornate facades and opulent interiors of palaces, museums, theaters and parks. The author uses a popular style of writing, with pictures of gleaming ballrooms, libraries, and gardens of the tsars of Russia. Steve Raymer who is the author of the book St. Petersburg, is both writer and photographer.

What you have learned

This chapter covers material that instructors often find as peripherally valuable, self-explanatory, and easy to learn. The result is that most students do not know how to cite the work they use in their reports; do not give credit to ideas they use; do not appreciate the value of evidence which they need to consider in their writings and presentations; and above all, do not know how to evaluate a given work.

This chapter is by no means comprehensive and exhaustive. However, it is important that you start understanding the power of citing and critical reading of information sources. This chapter has introduced you to the following terms and concepts. We gloss over only the most important terminology:

Archival sources   Information contained in personal papers, diaries, photo albums, and logs; manuscripts, drawings, and sketches; first editions, cultural artifacts, and other unique objects.

Bibliographic citation   A record in precise and consistent form that gives details about an item used in your work regardless of its format and medium; the item is typically identified and described with the following data elements: author's name, title, physical description, subject headings, and availability. Other data may include call number, price, and Internet address.

Bibliographic style manual	A document that offers guidance to writers on how to consistently cite works which are used in their writings. There are many different styles of citing printed and online sources.
Data elements	Unitary pieces of information that make up a bibliographic record. Examples include author's name, title, source where that item is published, and date of publication.
Formal communication	Recorded pieces of knowledge that are peer-reviewed (critically reviewed by a panel of experts on the accounts of content and style) and published in books, periodical literature, and audiovisual works.
Informal communication	Defined as information that is transmitted through informal channels such as phone, fax, face-to-face dialog, e-mail, and other archival data.
Primary sources	Pertaining to documents and art objects that contain novel ideas in humanities, social sciences, and sciences/engineering, new methods, and applications. Examples are: fiction, patents, films, and sound recordings.
Secondary sources	Reference sources that are designed, through their structure, to rapidly give you needed information or reference to primary sources. Examples are library catalogs and online magazine databases.
Summary (annotation)	A summary, often called an abstract or annotation tells us what the document says. Depending on the nature of the document, content and format of the annotation may vary.

Annotated Bibliography

Introduction

We have annotated a selected body of literature that relates to various aspects of information literacy. Teachers and librarians who are already offering IL skills to their high school students will find many well-known writers and IL models throughout this bibliography. Others, who are thinking about designing their own programs, may find this bibliography useful as a survey of contributors from many different disciplines: librarians and educators, psychologists, and other researchers.

Mainly, we have searched the ERIC database, and other library and information science online databases that are available through the Dialog retrieval system. These include: *Library & Information Science Abstracts* (LISA, file 61), *Psychological Abstracts* (file 11), *and Information Science Abstracts* (file 202). We have also used other reports and the extensive personal files on this topic.

This bibliography is organized under the following five headings:

- Selected publications by the American Library Association.
- Information literacy models.
- From question to assessment.
- Information seeking: children's use of Internet resources.
- Critical thinking.

1. The American Library Association position on information literacy

American Association of School Librarians. (1994). *Information Literacy: A position statement on information problem solving.* Chicago : The American Association of School Librarians. The Web address: <http://www.ala.org/aasl/positions/PS_infolit.html>.
The term Information Literacy, according to AASL, is applied to the skills of information problem-solving. The purpose of AASL position paper "is to identify the key elements of information literacy and present a rationale for integrating information literacy into all aspects of the K-12 and post-secondary curriculum. Many aspects of both the school restructuring movement and library media programs relate to information literacy and its impact on student learning."

American Association of School Librarians and Association for Educational Communications and Technology. (1998). *Information Power: Building Partnership for Learning.* Chicago : American Library

Association. This book builds on contributions by the American Library Association in the area of guidelines and standards for K-12 school libraries. Organized into two parts, the book first lays out three major areas (learning and teaching; information access; and program administration), nine standards, and 29 indicators. Part Two consists of five chapters, each discussing important components of information literacy. For example, Chapter 2 introduces Collaboration, Leadership, and Technology. Chapter 4 through 6 cover the school library media program's main responsibilities of Learning and Teaching, Information Access and Delivery, and Program Administration. Chapter 7 includes Connections to the Learning Community.

2. Information literacy models

Classical information retrieval systems (IRS) were predominantly computer-centered and based on the premise that searchers' information needs represented in the form of precise query would match documents represented in the form of document surrogates and produce the end result. Furthermore, IRS in the pre-digital library era were designed with little or no sensitivity toward the user. As demonstrated in the reported studies below, there is a space for the design of better IRS that are usable by ordinary people, including children. One way to design user-centered IRS, especially in the digital context, is to look at how people, especially children, seek and search for information. We rarely see children searching in five or six or 10 or any fixed number of clear-cut steps in order to get information they need. Search experience is a more random process in which people accomplish their goal through a series of exploratory and repetitive moves. Children constantly shift their focus as their knowledge evolves; they prefer pictorial and multimedia rich contents rather than print and bibliographic sources. They also incorporate feelings into their search process. Some of these information seeking models have been reported in selected studies below. Not only is it fascinating to learn about information seeking among children at different stages of their cognitive and physical development, but this knowledge can serve as a framework to designing richer and more sensitive IRS than it has been possible so far.

Bates, Marcia. J. (October 1989). The design of browsing and berrypicking techniques for the online search interface. *Online Review*, 13 (5): 407-424.
The proposed information-seeking model goes away from the traditional linear model in which a single search query is put into a system with the expectation of a relevant outcome. In contrast, Bates sees the search process as a constantly evolving strategy in which searching and browsing techniques support one another.

Eisenberg, Michael B. and Robert E. Berkowitz. (1995). The six habits of highly effective students. *School Library Journal,* 41(8): 22-25.

The authors of "The Big Six" approach to information problem-solving identify the following six "skills that are transferable to school, personal, and work applications, as well as all subject areas across a full range of grade levels" (p. 23) These are: 1. Task definition (define the problem; identify the information need); 2. Information seeking strategies (brain-storm all possible sources; select the best sources); 3. Location and access (locate sources intellectually/physically); 4. Use of information (read, hear, view, and extract relevant information); 5. Synthesis (organize information from multiple sources, and present the results); and 6. Evaluation (judge the result, and judge the process).

Ercegovac, Zorana. (1995). Interpretation access instruction (IAI4): Design principles. *College & Research Libraries,* 56(3): 249-257.

This article proposes four design principles — *The User, Active Learning, Conceptual Model of Teaching, Modularity* — as a conceptual framework of an Information Access Instruction (**IAI** [4]). These principles, when put in practice as specific guidelines, seamlessly link information sources together regardless of their implementation medium, information struc-ture, or interface style. Examples are drawn from a section that was designed by the author of a four-unit elective undergraduate course and taught at the University of California, Los Angeles (1991-1998).

Ercegovac, Zorana. (1997). The interpretation of library use in the age of digital libraries: Virtualizing the name. *Library & Information Science Research,* 19(1): 31-46.

To study the extent to which students interpret the term library use, the author gathered answers by means of a questionnaire in a sample of 57 upper-division undergraduates at UCLA. The concept of *library use* was operationalized with 22 well-established library activities. These activities define library as a SPACE, as a STORE, and as a SERVICE. The study suggests that the notion of the library as a *space* is better agreed upon than the notion of the library as a *store* or *service.* To understand potential sources for this ambiguity, the study looks at the traditional model of libraries. Then, the transition from the traditional library model to the dig-ital one is analyzed using five paradigm shifts.

Ercegovac, Zorana. (1998). *Information Literacy: Search Strategies, Tools & Resources 7-12 (ST&R 7-12).* Los Angeles: InfoEN Associates.

This book preceded *Information Literacy: Search Strategies, Tools & Resources for High School Students* (Ercegovac, 2001).

Kuhlthau, Carol C. (Feb/Mar 1999a). Accommodating the user's information search process: Challenges for information retrieval system designers. *Bulletin of the American Society for Information Science*, 25(3): 12-16.

Information seeking, according to Kuhlthau, "incorporates the experience of interactive thoughts, actions, and feeling in the process of construction." (pp. 8-9) Thoughts relate to the cognitive domain, such as problem solving; actions relate to the sensorimotor domain such as scrolling and navigating through the Web; and feelings relate to the affective domain, such as uncertainty, clarity, interests, likes (dislikes), motivation, and so on. The affective dimension of the information search process (ISP) has been explored, especially in the area of children's searching and seeking, in Kuhlthau's research. Her description of the ISP model has been published in a series of studies, some of which are included in this bibliography.

Kuhlthau, Carol C. (1993). *Seeking meaning: A process approach to library and information services.* Norwood, N.J. : Ablex.

Kuhlthau, Carol C. (1997). Learning in digital libraries: An information search process. *Library Trends*, 45, 708-724.

Kuhlthau, Carol C. (1999b). The role of experience in the information search process of an early career information worker: Perceptions of uncertainty, complexity, construction, and sources. *Journal of the American Society for Information Science*, 50(5): 399-412.

Pitts, Judy M. (Spring 1995). Mental models of information: The 1993-94 AASL/Highsmith Research Award study. *School Library Media Quarterly*, 23 (3): 177-184.

The purpose of the research was to investigate the question of when students are seeking and using information, why do they make the decisions they make. The article presents findings of the research and offers suggestions to educators who are planning a learning experience.

Stripling, Barbara K. (Spring 1995). Learning-centered libraries: Implications from research. *School Library Media Quarterly*, 23 (3): 163-170.

The article is an interpretation and implication of Judy Pitts' research for practice. The main idea is that library programs must be based around learning and not around libraries. Learning is viewed as a process that involves constructing mental models, and consisting of the content strand (need to know/concept and essential questions; information; new understanding; and assessment product) and process strand (inquiry; synthesis/decision making; and expression). Learning is seen as a recursive process.

3. **From question to assessment**

Bertland, Linda H. (Winter 1986). An overview of research in metacognition: Implications for information skills instruction. *School Library Media Quarterly*, pp. 96-99.
Describes research conducted on the development of metacognition, the process, by which people evaluate the act of thinking, in a number of areas such as attention, memory, linguistics, and social cognition focusing on these areas that bear most closely upon children's use of the library: their ability to monitor their comprehension of information and to develop and use appropriate strategies. The implications of metacognitive research, while important in learning and in the design of information literacy programs, has been little studied compared to, for example, critical thinking, problem solving, and collaboration. More research is needed on the processes of metacognition, and in the effectiveness of programs designed to teach students the metacognitive skills. Metacognition, both for students and teachers, should be an integral part of any IL program.

For the **CRESST** cognitive model of learning, reader is referred to a series of reports and excellent bibliographies by Eva L. Baker and her colleagues at the *Center for the Study of Evaluation, National Center for Research on Evaluation, Standards, and Student Testing* (CRESST). Graduate School of Education & Information Studies at the University of California Los Angeles, Los Angeles.

Chung, Gregory K. W. K., Herl, Howard E., Davina C. D. Klein, O'Neil Harold F. Jr., & John Schacter. (December 1997). Estimate of the potential costs and effectiveness of scaling up CRESST assessment software. CSE Technical Report 462. Center for the Study of Evaluation, *National Center for Research on Evaluation, Standards, and Student Testing*. Graduate School of Education & Information Studies at the University of California Los Angeles, Los Angeles.

Doyle, Christina S. (June 24, 1992). *Outcome measures for information literacy within the National Education Goals of 1990. Final Report to National Forum on Information Literacy. Summary of Findings.* (ED 351 033).
Representatives from 46 national organizations created a comprehensive definition of information literacy and developed outcome measures for the concept. The top three outcome measures were as follows: (1) All children should start school ready to learn. (2) Elementary and secondary school

students need to learn how to learn in order to make informed decisions. (3) Adults must be provided with the literacy and other skills necessary for employment and citizenship.

Feinberg, R. and C. King. (1992). Performance evaluation in bibliographic instruction workshop courses: assessing what students do as a measure of what they know. *Reference Services Review*, 20 (2): 75-80. The BI program at the state University of New York (BI) at Stony Brook features four undergraduate courses that utilize workbooks and workshops to teach students basic library skills. Teacher observation and evaluation of students' performance are major course elements. The paper concludes that despite difficulties related to observational evaluation procedures, these courses are advantageous to students.

Fry, Thomas K. and Joan Kaplowitz. (Summer 1988). The English 3 library instruction program at UCLA: a follow-up study. *Research Strategies*, 6 (3): 100-108. Students' library usage, attitudes, and skills were surveyed three years after the students had participated in a library instruction program at University of California at Los Angeles. The survey design was based on one previously used for the evaluation carried out during the program's first year. The scores of the 100 survey participants compared favorably to those of students surveyed three weeks after being involved in the original program.

Gross, Melissa. (Spring 1997). Pilot study on the prevalence of imposed queries in a school library media center. *School Library Media Quarterly*, 25 (3): 157-165. Gross asks the question, "what is the prevalence of imposed queries (versus self-generated) in the school library media center." The paper identifies and describes individual stages of development in the imposed query. The investigator categorized imposed queries by gender and by user level (i.e., early childhood, primary, middle, upper, teacher, parent). The study found that the number of imposed queries was higher at the upper grade level and that personal use was lowest among the older children. In addition, 87 percent of the imposed queries were attributed to teacher assignments.

Houghton, Janaye M. and Robert S. Houghton. (1999). *Decision Points: Boolean Logic for Computer Users and Beginning Online Searchers*. Englewood, CO: Libraries Unlimited. This book clarifies search concepts, and search strategies; it is written for educators who use the technique of Boolean logic (AND, OR, NOT) in online searching. The book includes worksheets that are reproducible, an answer key to activities, table of selected Boolean features, and an index.

Kaplowitz, Joan. (Winter 1986). A pre- and post-test evaluation of the English 3-library instruction program at UCLA. *Research Strategies*, 4 (1): 111-17.
Pre- and post-tests were administered to approximately one-third of the students who participated in the University of California at Los Angeles Library's English 3-Library Instruction Program. The program's effect on the students library-related behavior was evaluated. Changes in library usage, attitude toward libraries and librarians, and understanding of basic library skills were studied. Statistical analysis of the data indicated that students scored significantly higher on the post-test than on the pre-test. This suggests that the program benefited those students enrolled and is an efficient and effective way of offering bibliographic instruction to all students at UCLA.

Kuhlthau, Carol C., Ed. (1994). *Assessment and the School Library Media Center*. Boulder, Co.: Libraries Unlimited, Inc.
Assessment of student learning, the measuring of students' progress and performance, is an important concern for library media specialists.
Twelve articles are presented which address the issue of assessment of library media services. The titles are: "The Growth of Assessment" (George F. Madaus, Ann G. A. Tan); "Library Information Skills and Standardized Achievement Tests" (Mary M. Jackson); "From Indicators of Quantity to Measures of Effectiveness: Ensuring 'Information Power's' Mission" (Robert E. Berkowitz); "Expanding the Evaluation Role in the Critical-Thinking Curriculum" (Daniel Callison); "Assessing the Library Research Process." (Carol Collier Kuhlthau); "Alternative Assessment: Promises and Pitfalls" (Delia Neuman); "Assessment of Student Performance: The Fourth Step in the Instructional Design Process" (Barbara K. Stripling); "What's the Difference between 'Authentic' and 'Performance' Assessment?" (Carol A. Meyer); "Practicing Authentic Assessment in the School Library" (Barbara K. Stripling); "The Potential for Portfolio Assessment" (Daniel Callison); "Assessing the Big Outcomes" (Nora Redding); and "Linking Assessment to Accountability: Sixth-Grade Performance Assessment" (Willa Spicer, Joyce Sherman).

O'Neil, Harold F., Jr. and Jamal Abedi. (1996). Reliability and validity of a state metacognitive inventory: Potential for alternative assessment. Center for Student Evaluation (CSE) Technical Report 469. Los Angeles: CRESST. Excellent bibliography. The report is published as a journal article in 1996 in *Journal of Educational Research*, 89, pp. 234-245.

The reported research found that the construct validity of state metacognitive inventory (SMI) yields useful information about both the assessment and high school students. SMI is not recommended for 8th grade students or lower than 8th grade. State metacognitive inventory relates to those intellectual situations that are characterized by planning, organization, self-monitoring, and cognitive strategies; in contrast, traits inventory pertains to stable individual difference variable such as intelligence and aptitude.

Stanley, Deborah B. (1999). *Practical Steps to the Research Process for High School.* Information Literacy Series. Englewood, CO: Libraries Unlimited.
This guide to the *Research Process* at the high school level is a four-day diary of research lessons. The main assumption is collaboration. The four sections of this book cover: 1. Planning and preparation; 2. The research process; 3. Application and accountability; 4. Enrichment and extension. The book includes figures, references, and an index.

Walter, Virginia A. (1992). *Output measures for public library service to children: A manual of standardized procedures.* Chicago : American Library Association.
The author in her introduction writes that the manual is a practical guide to quantifying and measuring the results, or outputs, of public library service to children, defined as people of 14 years of age or younger and their care givers. (p. 1). The Manual contains sources for additional information, examples and illustrations, forms for data collection, as well as blank forms for material logs, work sheets, surveys, both in English and Spanish.

4. Information seeking: children's use of Internet resources

The fourth group of studies has looked at information seeking behavior of children in elementary, middle and high schools, as they interact with electronic sources, especially the Internet. Each study contains an extensive selection of cited studies in their respective bibliographies.

Bilal, Dania. (2000). Children's use of the Yahooligans! Web search engine: I. Cognitive, physical, and affective behaviors on fact-based search tasks. *Journal of the American Society for Information Science*, 51(7): 646-665.
Bilal investigated cognitive, affective, and physical behaviors as 22 seventh-grade children (from a middle school in Knoxville, TN) searched the Yahooligans! search engine on a specific search task. The author concluded that the quality of the success was "influenced by four main factors:

(1) Novice Web navigational skills, (2) limited knowledge of using Yahooligans!, (3) Yahooligans! system design, and (4) the structure of hypermedia." (p. 661)

Fidel, Raya, et al. (1999) A visit to the information mall: Web searching behavior of high school students. *Journal of the American Society for Information Science*, 50(1): 24-37.
Fidel and her seven library students at the University of Washington, used field observations, students' verbal protocols ("thinking aloud" technique), and interviews to analyze Web searching behavior of high school students as they searched for their homework assignment. Students were satisfied with their search process and results, especially because the Web retrieved pictures, covered many topics, and was easy to access; students found response time to be too slow.

Hirsh, Sandra G. (1999). Children's relevance criteria and information seeking on electronic resources. *Journal of the American Society for Information Science*, 50(14): 1265-1283.
Hirsh used qualitative research methods to study how 10 fifth-grade children, randomly selected from a classroom at an elementary school in Tucson, Arizona, searched four different electronic sources (e.g., online catalog, electronic encyclopedia, magazine index, and the Web) on a single class assignment. The investigator identified a total of 254 mentions of relevance criteria. Searchers were interested more in pictures and little concerned for the authority of the retrieved work.

Kafai, Yasmin and Marcia J. Bates (Winter 1997). Internet Web-searching instruction in the elementary classroom: building a foundation for information literacy. *School Library Media Quarterly*, 25(2): 103-111.
The study reported on searching the Web by elementary school children, and then building children's information literacy skills. The objective of this study was to have children develop an understanding of what the Internet and web searching are, gain some skills in searching, and develop their critical-thinking skills by evaluating the information they gathered from various sites.

5. Critical thinking

Beyer, Barry K. (April 1985). Critical thinking: What is it? *Social Education*, 49(4): 270-76.
This article defines critical thinking as the process of determining the authenticity, accuracy, and worth of information or knowledge claims. It consists of a number of discrete skills.

Cornelio, Alicia. (Feb 1994). A multimedia approach to teaching library research skills. *School Library Media Activities Monthly*, 10(6): 38-40. The author describes activities and procedures that were developed to teach library research skills to grades five through eight using multimedia instruction, including the use of HyperStudio software. The paper discusses library media skills objectives, curriculum objectives, resources, instructional roles, hardware and software requirements, evaluation, and follow-up.

Drueke, Jeanetta. (Spring 1992). Active learning in the university library instruction classroom. *Research Strategies*, 10 (2): 77-83. Active learning techniques in elementary education and post-secondary education are discussed. The paper describes the successful conversion of a research methods lecture to an active learning session at the University of Nebraska library.

Krapp, JoAnn Vergona. (Jan 1988). Teaching research skills: A critical-thinking approach. *School Library Journal*, 34 (5): 32-35. The author reviews the literature of the critical thinking/problem solving approach to learning. The paper discusses how these concepts relate to teaching research skills. Two activities designed to teach critical thinking and research skills in the context of fifth and sixth grade social studies are summarized.

Wesley, Threasa. (Jan-Feb 1991). Teaching library research: Are we preparing students for effective information use? *Emergency Librarian*, 18 (3): 23-24, 26-30. When teaching library instruction mechanical skills are often presented first and little attention is given to the conceptual skills that are essential to successful library research. By refocusing instructional time to concentrate on decision making and evaluation, students can acquire library research competencies that will enable them to be effective information users. The paper suggests that topic analysis, consideration of the relevant perspectives, and choice of appropriate research guides, be the components of planning a research strategy. The author recommends that discriminating among available sources, and evaluating information sources, become the two aspects of choosing information sources.

Appendix A
The Dewey Decimal Classification

The Dewey Decimal Classification is © 1996–2000
OCLC Online Computer Library Center, Incorporated.
Used with Permission.
DDC, Dewey, and Dewey Decimal Classification are registered trademarks
of OCLC Online Computer Library Center, Incorporated.

000 GENERALITIES
010 Bibliographies & catalogs
020 Library & information sciences
030 General encyclopedic works
040 Unassigned
050 General serials & their indexes
060 General organizations & museology
070 News media, journalism, publishing
080 General collections
090 Manuscripts & rare books

100 PHILOSOPHY & PSYCHOLOGY
110 Metaphysics
120 Epistemology, causation, humankind
130 Paranormal phenomena
140 Specific philosophical schools
150 Psychology
160 Logic
170 Ethics (Moral philosophy)
180 Ancient, medieval, oriental philosophy
190 Modern Western philosophy

200 RELIGION
210 Natural theology
220 Bible
230 Christian theology
240 Christian moral & devotional theology
250 Christian orders & local churches
260 Christian social theology
270 Christian church history
280 Christian denominations & sects
290 Other and comparative religions

300 SOCIAL SCIENCES
    310 General statistics
    320 Political science
    330 Economics
    340 Law
    350 Public administration
    360 Social services; associations
    370 Education
    380 Commerce, communication, transport
    390 Customs, etiquette, folklore

400 LANGUAGE
    410 Linguistics
    420 English & old English
    430 Germanic languages
    440 Romance languages
    450 Italian, Romanian, Rhaeto-Romanic languages
    460 Spanish & Portuguese languages
    470 Italic languages, i.e., Latin
    480 Hellenic languages, i.e., Classical Greek
    490 Other languages

500 NATURAL SCIENCES & MATHEMATICS
    510 Mathematics
    520 Astronomy & allied sciences
    530 Physics
    540 Chemistry & allied sciences
    550 Earth sciences
    560 Paleontology, Paleozoology
    570 Life sciences
    580 Botanical sciences
    590 Zoological sciences

600 TECHNOLOGY (Applied Sciences)
    610 Medical sciences
    620 Engineering & allied sciences
    630 Agriculture
    640 Management & auxiliary services
    650 Chemical engineering
    660 Home economics & family living
    670 Manufacturing
    680 Manufacture for specific uses
    690 Buildings

700 THE ARTS

710 Civic & landscape art
720 Architecture
730 Plastic arts
740 Drawing & decorative arts
750 Painting & paintings
760 Graphic arts
770 Music
780 Photography & photographs
790 Recreational & performing arts

800 LITERATURE & RHETORIC

810 American literature in English
820 English and Old English literature
830 Literatures of Germanic languages
840 Literatures of Romance languages
850 Italian, Romanian, Rhaeto-Romanic
860 Spanish & Portuguese literatures
870 Italic literatures, i.e., Latin
880 Hellenic literatures, i.e., Classical Greek
890 Literatures of other languages

900 GEOGRAPHY & HISTORY

910 Geography & travel
920 Biography, Genealogy, Insignias
930 History of the ancient world
940 General history of Europe
950 General history of Asia & Far East
960 General history of Africa
970 General history of North America
980 General history of South America
990 General history of other areas

Appendix B

Acceptable Use Agreement:
(Your school name) Library Network/Internet

Internet access is available, through the library and computer lab, to the students, faculty, and staff of (your school name) School. We provide a variety of diverse information to the (your school name) community. We will now offer numerous excellent online services over the Web, such as *Encyclopedia Britannica* and *ProQuest*.

There will also be available material that is **not** considered educational. (Your school name) School has taken precautions to restrict access to obscene and illegal material: browsers at each workstation do not allow FTP (file transfer), Telnet (access to remote software), or news groups (online chatting with other remote computers). We will take all precautions possible; however, on a global network, it is impossible to control all materials. We believe the valuable information and interaction available far outweigh the possibility that users may procure information that is not consistent with the educational goals of the school. Users are expected to undertake responsibility for their research and to adhere to the standards outline in the **(your school name) School Student Guidelines** document they have signed. Outlined below are terms and conditions for the use of the (your school name) School Library network.

The guidelines are provided here so that you are aware of the responsibilities you are about to undertake. The responsibilities include: efficient, ethical, and legal utilization of network resources. If a user violates any of these provisions, his or her account may be terminated. Discretionary actions will also result. **The signatures at the end of this document are legally binding and indicate the parties who signed have read the terms and conditions carefully and understand their significance.**

Internet Terms and Conditions

Acceptable use:

Internet access to (your school name) Library has been provided to support research and education. You will be provided with a user login, which will allow you access to library databases (*ProQuest, NewsBank, Encyclopedia Britannica*, etc.), Internet sites, and file storage on the network. You are to use your account for purposes of education and research only. You may not download programs from the Internet, nor may you access or download video games, online auctions, or pornography at any time. If, during your research you encounter another organization's network, you must comply with the rules set out by that network. Transmission of any material in violation of any US or state regulation is prohibited. This includes, but is not limited to: copyrighted material, threatening or pornographic material, or material protected by trade secret. Use for product advertisement or political lobbying is also prohibited.

Vandalism is defined as any malicious attempt to harm or destroy materials or data belonging to another user, the (your school name) Library network, or any of the other networks to which (your school name) is connected. This includes, but is not limited to: uploading, downloading or the creation of computer viruses; altering and/or configuring the monitor settings; deliberately debilitating computer hardware, software or communication network; removing parts of the mouse balls and keyboards; and defacing or destroying library property (e.g., books, journals, furniture, computer related material of any kind). Vandalism will result in disciplinary action including suspension or cancellation of library and computer privileges.

Privileges:

The use of the (your school name) School Library and its services, including Internet access, is a privilege, not a right, and inappropriate use will result in the suspension or cancellation of those privileges. The Library staff may close an account at any time, as required.

Network etiquette: -)

- Be courteous.
- Use appropriate language—do not swear, use vulgarities or any other inappropriate language. Illegal activities are strictly forbidden.
- Do not reveal your password, login name or that of any other person.
- Do not use the network in such a way as to disrupt the use of the network by others.
- All communication and information accessible via the network should be presumed private property.
- Be economical with your time online so as not to unnecessarily slow down the connection.

Security:

The system's security is a high priority. If you can identify a security problem within the network or on the Internet, you must notify the Library Director, technology coordinator or your teacher at once. Do not demonstrate the problem to other users. Do not use another user's account. Attempts to login to the network as anyone other than yourself may result in immediate cancellation of privileges. You must log out of the network when you are finished. Any user identified as a security risk or having a history of problems with other computer systems may be denied access to the Library network and Internet access.

(Your library name) Library Network/Internet: Acceptable Use Agreement

Student

I understand and will abide by the *(your school library) Library Network/Internet: Acceptable Use Agreement.* I understand that any violation of the regulations is unethical and may constitute a criminal offense. Should I commit a violation, revocation of network access, disciplinary or legal action may occur.

User Name (please print): _____

User Signature: _____ Date: _____

Parent or guardian

(If you are under the age of 18, a parent or guardian must also read and sign this agreement)

As the parent or guardian of this student, I have read (your school library) Library Network/Internet: *Acceptable Use Agreement.* I understand that this access is designed for educational purposes. (Your school name) School has taken precautions, through education and software configuration, to eliminate access to illegal and age- inappropriate materials, defined as such sources—but not limited to—sexually explicit images and texts, information about drugs and the tools of violence, and instructions and programs to manipulate computers and networks without authorization. However, I also recognize that it is impossible for (your school name) School to restrict access to all illegal material and I will not hold them responsible for the quality or accuracy of materials acquired on the network. Further, I accept responsibility for supervision if and when my child's use is not within the School setting. I hereby give permission to issue an account for my child.

Parent or Guardian Name: (please print) _____

Parent or Guardian Signature: _____ Date: _____

Daytime telephone number: _____ Evening: _____

E-mail: _____

Library Director: _____

Signature: _____

Telephone number: _____ E-mail: _____

Appendix C
Lesson Plans:
Examples for Collaborative Projects

CURRICULUM (CONTENT) STANDARDS: find the content standards that apply to your state and school.

> **Example:** State of California, State Board of Education. History/Social science Content Standards, Grades K-12 <http://www.cde.ca.gov/board/board.html>. Accordingly, students in grades 9-12 demonstrate the following intellectual, reasoning, reflection and research skills:

- Chronological and spatial thinking
- Historical research, evidence and point of view
- Historical interpretation

> **Project Title** (example): The Roots of the Modern World

OBJECTIVES (example):
1. Students relate to the political, cultural, moral, military, economic, and legal principles in ancient Greece and Rome to the development of Western political thought.
2. Students learn to plan their research, locate, search, evaluate, organize information from multiple sources.
3. Students learn to collaborate on presentations of their work (preparation of quilts, visuals, advertisement brochures); students can present their work using different technologies, including Web pages on the intranet, PowerPoint presentation.
4. Students learn to peer review their work (scoring and evaluation criteria).

PROCEDURE (example):
1. Organize students into small teams of 2-4 students per each team.
2. Each team selects a significant track in Greece and Rome for its project (e.g., education; moral philosophy; manifestations of democracy).
3. Each group collects multiple sources, evaluates them, gives credit, annotates, and uses the information for their presentation.
4. Each team will teach others about the most significant contribution of their choice.
5. Each group prepares the three most significant readings and hands them out to other students ahead of time.

6. Students, as a group, read suggested references, and each team prepares one question for the presenter.
7. Teams prepare reports in their chosen formats, media, and technologies.
8. Each member of the team plays a different role: a facilitator in presenting, library guru, technology expert.
9. Teams work on critiquing and developing their own scoring criteria in order to rank the three best projects in class. The bibliography is an important part of the project.

RUBRICS:

Teachers and media specialists develop and test rubrics for:
- Research process, evaluation of sources.
- Management planning and execution of the research process.
- Writing (composition, grammar, creativity, the form).
- Presentation (the use of technology, speaking skills, time management, listening skills).
- Bibliography (style, accuracy and completeness).

RESOURCES:

The instructional team will select seed sources and put them on reserve. In addition, students will be introduced to a variety of sources in different media and formats. Students will develop their own specialized readings as a part of their research process.

INSTRUCTION TO STUDENTS:

The instructional team will distribute to students written instructions with clear objectives of the assigned project, tasks that need to be accomplished, deadlines, and evaluation criteria.

Some of the examples for standard-based instructional plans are:

Grade level	English Social	Studies	Science
10th grade	• Study of Julius Caesar by Shakespeare: "All roads lead to Rome" www.esc2.net/ TIELevel2/projects/ rome/	"RussianQuest?" by P.K. Muench: www.oswega.org/ staff/pmuench/ webquest/ russiaquest.html	Physics Multimedia http://www. glenbrook.k12.il. us/gbssci/phys/ mmedia/index. html

Content Knowledge and Grade Level

CURRICULUM (CONTENT) STANDARDS:

Project Title:

OBJECTIVES of the assigned project:

PROCEDURE:

RUBRICS:
Teachers and media specialists develop and test rubrics for:

RESOURCES:

INSTRUCTION TO STUDENTS:

Appendix D
Pre-Test: A baseline for Information Literacy Skills

Student's name (please print): _____

Pretend you are getting ready for your trip to _____.
You own a good map of the city.

Besides the map, what else do you need to know about your trip?
List the most important three things (for you) that you would want to know.

How would you go about finding it?

_____

1Q (I'd need/like to know ....):

1A Where would you find this information?

2Q (I'd like to know…):

2A Where would you find this information?

3Q (I'd like to …):

3A Where would you find this information?

Please return this sheet with your answers to me

THANK YOU

Appendix E
Scoring Rubrics: Examples for Information Literacy Projects

Score Point	CRITERIA FOR SCORING INFORMATION LITERACY
4	**Exceeds expectations**

4   **Exceeds expectations**

Student identifies at least five main topics (see list of topics on the next page).

Student shows understanding of content knowledge for each topic.

Student demonstrates depth of understanding (e.g., uses specific facts, examples, vocabulary).

All topics are described or discussed accurately.

Vocabulary is used accurately.

Related information is connected (e.g., credit giving).

The writing is organized around main ideas.

Student gives insights/observations of his/her own.

Answers are well written.

Student is creative in presentation and title page selection.

There are few spelling errors.

3   **Meets expectations**

Student identifies at least three to four main topics (see list of topics on the next page).

Student shows understanding of content knowledge for each topic.

All topics are described and discussed accurately.

Related information is connected (e.g., credit giving).

Student's writing skills needs some improvement; the message is clear.

There are a number of spelling errors.

2   **Close to expectations**

Student identifies at least three topics.

Student shows understanding of content knowledge for each topic.

Student demonstrates depth of understanding.
All topics are described and discussed accurately.
Student's writing skills needs major improvement (revision, etc.).
There are a number of spelling errors, grammatical problems, etc.

1   **Does not meet expectations**
Student demonstrates little content understanding; lists two topics and misses major ones.
Student gives some inaccurate and / or irrelevant answers or examples.
Student has numerous problems with writing, spelling, and structure.

■ Information Literacy major topics, below, are presented over a five-to-seven-week period for two hours a week.

1. Finding books in library; classification and DDC.
2. Search strategies, revisited.
3. Search modification.
4 Data elements in catalog entry.
5. Differences between subject headings and keyword searching.
6. Searching library catalogs.
7. Use of encyclopedias (uses and importance in research).
8. Variety of printed sources.
9. The Web, its use, evaluation.
10. Practice of citing (writing bibliographies; understanding plagiarism).
11. Evaluation.
12. Library rules, Fair Use Policy.
13. Research practice and general rules of thumb.

■ Instructional strategies: short lecture followed by a project-based, guided hands-on collaborative activities in small teams of two students in a group. Setting is the computer lab.

■ Materials: ST&R7-12 book, companion software, problem-based in-class assignments (project related), three open-book short quizzes, one final take-home project.

■ Goals: to introduce students in the research process and the use of quality and diversity of sources in their own work (e.g., finding, evaluating, citing, managing, asking questions).

Appendix F
Post-Test: An Example for Take Home Final Quiz

Imagine your cousin Sara visits you from Maryland. You want to explain to her what you learned in your information literacy component of History class.

Write an essay that includes information literacy topics that every 9th grade student should learn and know. You may want to select the most important and interesting topics to you that we have covered in our classes. Since this is a take home assignment, you may use any material to help you write the essay (as you did during the open book quizzes in school).

Instructions:
Make a front cover and include the following two things:
- Give a title to your essay paper.
- Put your name (last and first) on the front cover.

Instructions for the essay:
- You may want to type your paper and run a spellcheck before you turn in.
- The paper should be at least one full page and not more than three pages in length.
- You can include bibliography: one to two entries at the end of your paper.
- Write clearly using full sentences; write your essay into several paragraphs: an idea = one paragraph. Be imaginative and have fun!

Appendix G
Metacognition:
Questions to help teachers get insight into students' level of awareness

Metacognitive skills consist of questions intended to assess students' awareness and perception of the level of planning, cognitive strategy, self-checking, and awareness during a problem solving task (O'Neil & Abedi). These questions are given to students in testing situations, and may be extended to Web searching, research report preparation, and similar situations.

> Planning
> Cognitive strategy
> Self-Checking
> Awareness

The following sets of questions (O'Neil & Abedi) are grouped into the four types of metacognition. Each set of questions is then linked to applications that are specific to information literacy tasks.

> **Planning**
> I tried to understand the goals of the test questions before I attempted to answer.
> I tried to determine what the test required.
> I made sure I understood just what had to be done and how to do it.
> I determined how to solve the test questions.
> I tried to understand the test questions before I attempted to solve them.

Application to IL tasks:
Most of the high school students are assigned class projects (GOAL) that they need to achieve and produce by certain time on a specified topic(s). The teacher typically hands out the assigned project (take home test, term paper) in a form of a written requirement that students need to meet. **Means** to achieve the goal are not specified.

The **Planning** consists first of understanding what exactly is required before investing time and effort (going to library, spending time to locate, read, take notes, analyze, evaluate, cite, etc.). Second, the overall research planning is needed as a blueprint of what will actually be done in the research process. At this point, students might want to get the teachers' approval before they proceed with their research process. Once the plan is approved of, students will design a more detailed plan in order to find and locate the best information sources for the assigned project. Search strategy as well as the roadmap in Figure 1.7 may help in the planning phase

---

Cognitive Strategy
I attempted to discover the main ideas in the questions.
I asked myself how the test questions related to what I already knew.
I thought through the meaning of the test questions before I began to answer them.
I used multiple thinking techniques or strategies to solve the test question.
I selected and organized relevant information to solve the test questions.

Application to IL:
■ What are the substrategies for specific systems?
■ What do I need to have and know in order to search library catalog (vocabulary of the domain knowledge; conceptual preparation; mechanics of searching specific systems—they are all different; do I use connectors and which ones?)

Self-Checking
I checked my work while I was doing it.
I corrected my errors.
I almost always knew how much of the test I had left to complete.
I kept track of my progress and, if necessary, I changed my techniques or strategies.
I checked my accuracy as I progressed through the test.

Application to IL:
■ How am I doing? (both print, online, the Web)?
■ Any good cites (exploit those and get more good cites)?

- Getting zero results—what does that mean? Which errors did I make?
- How can I fix these errors? What types of errors? Typographic errors, wrong words, wrong syntax, wrong database?
- Do I know where I am, what I am searching (content)?
- Do I need to modify my search: narrow down, or expand search to get more results?

Awareness
- I was aware of my thinking.
- I was aware of which thinking technique or strategy to use and when to use it.
- I was aware of the need to plan my course of action.
- I was aware of my ongoing thinking process.
- I was aware of my trying to understand the test questions before I attempted to solve them.

Appendix H
Online Databases: A Checklist for Evaluating Online Services

This Appendix has two parts: Part One contains a checklist that librarians and teachers can use as a tool for evaluating, comparing, and contrasting online database services. Part Two briefly summarizes *ProQuest*, *NewsBank*, and *SirS* services. This certainly is a partial list of online database services that many schools consider and subscribe to.

Part One: Checklist for evaluating web-ready online databases for schools

1. Scope and sense of one's space in a given system.

   1.1   What is the breadth of the database? For example, how many journals, newspapers, and magazines are regularly indexed in the database?

   1.2   What is the depth of the database? For example, how many scholarly periodical titles are included? Are there any of popular nature, of technical orientation?

   1.3   What else is included in the database? Examples may be reference books, reports, and if so, who produces them?

   1.4   What is the time coverage of the database or parts of it?

   1.5   How current is the database? Some think that if the service is online that it is more current than printed services; this may not be true.

   1.6   Which languages are represented besides English? Examples may be Spanish, French newspapers, reports, and so forth.

   1.7   Is there a special description or explanation about inclusion policy and/or indexing policy? Can you as a teacher or librarian suggest materials to be included or considered in the database?

   1.8   How aligned is the content to middle school curriculum? To high school curriculum?

   1.9   How integrated is the content with regard to textbooks and standards for a particular grade level?

   1.10 Is the content self-explanatory?

2. Ease of using a given database.

    2.1   What kinds of tutorials are available for high school students?
    2.2   How much extra teaching do we have to invest in order to teach students in the use of a given database?
    2.3   Is the system (online database) forgiving? This may be viewed at several levels: typographic errors, syntax, reminders, and so forth.

3. User interface criteria (defined as anything that the user comes in contact with, physically, cognitively, perceptually).

    3.1   How well are the screens labeled?
    3.2   Is the layout designed consistently?
    3.3   Is the system free of library terminology (jargon)?

4. System complexity: access and vocabulary issues.
    4.1   How is database organized?
    4.2   Are there vocabulary lists that may be useful in searching?
    4.3   Is the level of specificity in subject lists useful to the high school students?
    4.4   How does the vocabulary list compare with the level of specificity of their project topics?

Part Two: Summary of *NewsBank* Resources for schools:

- Curriculum Resource By *NewsBank*
- *NewsBank* SchoolMate
- *SchoolMate* KidsPage
- *NewsBank* NewsFile Collection contains about 300,000 articles selected from over 500 newspapers and 10 newswires on topics, such as the arts, politics, sports, and more
- ScienceSource Collection
- Spanish Language Studies (Noticias en Espanol)
- Numerous full-length articles from original Spanish language news sources (not translations)
- Business Information provides about 130,000 articles annually with graphics
- *StatBank* includes historical data on more than 450 topics with international coverage
- Full-Text Newspaper Titles

The service is available online, via CD-ROM, or via NewsBank InfoWeb. There is a NewsBank Thesaurus as a controlled vocabulary list that may be used in subject searching.

397 Main Street, Chester, VT 05143
Telephone: (800) 243-7694
Fax: (802) 875-2904
Internet: <www.newsbank.com>

Summary of *SirS* Databases for schools:
SirS offers 4 main databases that can be purchased annually; these are:

- *SirS* **Researcher** is a general database that contains full-text articles from more than 1,200 publications worldwide. These are searchable by three search methods: by means of using Subject Headings Search, Topic Browse, and Keyword Search. The CD-ROM version contains excerpts from *The World Almanac and Book of Facts* (1998). There are maps as well. The Web version includes a dictionary and thesaurus and Today's News—headline news stories updated hourly.
- **SirS Discoverer** is an interactive reference tool for young researchers, with articles from more than 450 publications; this database is searchable via Subject Tree, Keyword Search and Subject Heading Search.
- **SirS Government Reporter** contains full-text government documents and recent U.S. Supreme Court decisions on a wide variety of topics. This database is searchable through Subject Tree Search, Subject Headings Search, Department/Agency Browse, Keyword Search, Country Profile Browse, and Census Bureau Browse.
- **SirS Renaissance** contains full-text articles from 500 sources in the Arts & Humanities. The database is cumulative and updated every February and September. Search methods include: Subject Tree, Subject Headings Search and Keyword Search.

All databases are available in the CD-ROM versions for Mac and Windows, as well as on the Web.
Telephone: (800) 232-SIRS
Fax: (561) 994-4704
Internet: <www.sirs.com>

Summary of *ProQuest* Database:
ProQuest's users can select from the main menu "all databases" or one of the following choices:

- Platinum periodicals with more than 2000 magazine and journal titles
- *ProQuest* Newspapers with *El Norte* and *Reforma*, Spanish language dailies from Mexico City
- International Newspapers with major English language papers
- *The New York Times*

- *Wall Street Journal*
- Reference sources include *World Book Encyclopedia*
- *Occupational Outlook Handbook*
- *The Ethnic Cultures of America*
- *The World Factbook* (Central Intelligence Agency)

As the other two services, *ProQuest* is available both on the CD-ROM and via the Internet. The database may be explored by 14 broad categories. It can also be searched in two different modes: the basic search option as well as the advanced. Please refer to Chapter 8 for details.

Telephone: (800) 889-3358

Outside the U.S. and Canada, call 1-734-761-4700

Internet: <http://proquest.umi.com>

Appendix I
Citing in Style

There are many different styles for citing sources used in your projects. We use:

Kate L. Turabian. 1996. *A manual for writers of term papers, theses, and dissertations.* 6th ed., rev by John Grossman and Alice Bennett. Chicago: University of Chicago Press.

This manual is written by a single author, Kate L. Turabian, now in its sixth edition; this edition is revised by two writers, namely, John Grossman and Alice Bennett.

The general format for a single author book is:

> Author's Last Name, <space> Author's First Name <space> Middle Initial. Date of publication. Title of book. <capitalize only the first words of the title and subtitle and any proper noun> Edition statement. <numbered, revised, enlarged> Place of Publication: Publisher's Name.

The same information, but according to a different bibliographic style, *The Publication Manual of the American Psychological Association* would look a bit differently. The general formula for APA style follows:

> Author's Last Name, <space> Author's First Name <space> Middle Initial. (Date of publication). Title of book. <capitalize only the first words of the title and subtitle and any proper noun> Place of Publication: Publisher's Name.

You get the picture. What is important is:

1. To give credit to works you use in your own writings.
2. To record complete and accurate information of works you are citing in your bibliography.
3. To choose a bibliographic style, such as Turabian's Manual, APA's Manual, MLA's Manual, and stick to its rules rather than to use different Manuals each time you compile a bibliography for your reports.

Basic formula for citing encyclopedia article from the printed version is:

> *Title of the Encyclopedia*, edition., s.v. (means that you looked under word) "name of the person/place/topic that you looked under."

Example:
Encyclopedia Britannica, 15th ed., s.v. "Hutchinson, Thomas."

The basic template for citing an encyclopedia article in its Web version is:

> "Title of the article," *Title of the Encyclopedia online*; accessed<date that you looked up>; available from < URL address >

Example:
"Adams Family," *Encyclopedia Britannica online*; accessed <October 20, 2000>; available from <http://www.eb.com>

Basic template to cite magazine articles is as follows:

> Last Name, First Name (Middle Initial, if given). Publication date. Title of the article. *Title of the Magazine* volume number (Month issued) : pages of your article.

If you replace the above data elements, the answer will be as follows:

> Bingham Hull, Jennifer. 1999. Can coffee drinkers save the rain forest. *Atlantic Monthly* 284 (August): 19–21.

The basic rule for using footnotes and endnotes follows:

Each time you cite a publication in your paper you should do the following two things:

1. In the paper: Identify your cited reference with a raised Arabic number half a space above the line.

Example:

In a recent article on the air we inhale, we read that "although Los Angeles has the most polluted skies in the nation, it is one of the few cities where air quality has improved in recent decades."[1]

2. Cite the source either at the foot of the page (FOOTNOTE) below a short line, or at the end of the paper (ENDNOTE). Example for the footnote:

---

[1]James M. Lents and William J. Kelly, Cleaning the air in Los Angeles, *Scientific American* 269 (1993): 32–39.

The template for citing Web documents is:

> Author's Last Name, First Name. "Title of Work," accessed <date>; available from <URL address>.

If you replace the above parts with the corresponding data from a Web page, your citations are as follows:

> Vandergrift, Kay E. "Vandergrift's children's literature page," accessed May 15, 1999; available from <http://www.scils.rutgers.edu/special/kay/childlit.html>.

There are numerous other cases that go beyond listing them all or most of them. Consult your teachers and librarians for suggestion as to which style to follow; then, purchase your own Manual as a reference source to use throughout your high school and college years, and beyond.

Appendix J
Summarizing Information Sources

There are four basic rules to remember whenever you annotate documents used in your reports:

■ Use your own words and not the authors' words. Making teeny changes, such as word variants, synonymous words and phrases, and changing word direction, does not count. These remain the authors' words. Teachers know how to recognize your language from your parents,' authors,' even your older brothers' and sisters.' So, stick to your own words and understanding of the work you wish to cite and include in your bibliography.

■ Mention highlights only rather than everything that is discussed in the document you are annotating. Separate important things from less important ones; be selective. If you are given two to three sentences only to summarize a work, what would it look like?

■ Be critical of others' writings in a positive way.

■ Include, as much as you wish, your own insight and understanding; make connections.

How to summarize (annotate) an article: an example

> Raymer, Steve. 1993. St. Petersburg, Capital of the Tsars. *National Geographic* 184 (6): 96-121.

Summary: St. Petersburg (also known as Petrograd, or City of Peter as well as Leningrad) is a monument to the worldly aspirations of its namesake rule and his imperial successors, has survived the communist years to rival Moscow as Russia's cultural center. The article also shows historical and city maps of the city. In terms of *organization*, the article is typical of other Magazine stories. It traces the city's rich and turbulent history since its birth in 1703, Russia's triumph over Napoleon in 1812, and the 1917 revolution. Special *features* are photographs of lavish mosaics gracing the Church of the Resurrection, ornate facades and opulent interiors of palaces, museums, theaters and parks. The author uses a popular style of writing, with pictures of gleaming ballrooms, libraries, and gardens of the tsars of Russia. Steve Raymer who is the author of the book St. Petersburg, is both writer and photographer.

Summarizing your Sources on Your Own

> Put your citation here

Summary:

Issues or questions the work raises:

Special features of the work (index, resources, illustrations, interviews, pictures, portraits, primary sources such as manuscripts and diaries, statistical tables):

Organization:

Currency, multiple perspectives presented, detected bias, evidence, references

How relevant is this work to your project (is the intended audience mentioned in the preface or introduction)?

Appendix K
Sources

Manuals of Bibliographic Style

Gibaldi, Joseph. *MLA Handbook for Writers of Research Papers*. 4th ed. New York: Modern Language Association of America, 1995.

Publication Manual of the American Psychological Association. 4th ed. Washington, DC: The Association, 1994.

Turabian, K. L. *A Manual for Writers of Term Papers, Theses, and Dissertations*. 6th ed. Rev. by John Grossman and Alice Bennett. Chicago: University of Chicago Press, 1996.

"Desk" or "College" Dictionaries

The American Heritage Dictionary of the English Language. 3rd ed. Boston: Houghton Mifflin, 1992.

Webster's Ninth New Collegiate Dictionary. Rev. ed. Springfield, Mass.: Merriam-Webster, 1990.

Unabridged Dictionaries

Oxford English Dictionary. J. Simpson and E. Sdmund Weiner, eds. 2d ed. Oxford: Clarendon Press, 1989, 20 vols. Supplements.

Webster's Third New International Dictionary. Springfield, Mass.: Merriam-Webster, 1993.

Subject or Technical Dictionaries

Allaby, M. *Dictionary of the Environment*. 3rd ed. New York: New York University Press, 1989.

Dorland's Illustrated Medical Dictionary. 29th ed. Philadelphia: W. B. Saunders, 2000.

New Grove Dictionary of Music and Musicians. Washington, DC.: Grove's Dictionaries of Music, 1980. 20 vols.

Slang Dictionaries

Chapman, Robert L., ed. *New Dictionary of American Slang*. New York: Harper & Collins, 1997.

Partridge, Eric. *Dictionary of Slang and Unconventional English*. 1st American ed. New York: Macmillan, 1990.

Synonyms and Antonyms
Roget's International Thesaurus. 5th ed. New York: HarperCollins, 1992.

General and Comprehensive Encyclopedias
The Encyclopedia Americana. The International ed. Danbury, Conn: Grolier, 1994, 30 vols.

The New Encyclopedia Britannica, 15th ed. Chicago: Encyclopedia Britannica, 1992, 32 vols.

World Book Encyclopedia. Chicago: World Book, 1997, 22 vols.

Subject Encyclopedias
McGraw-Hill Encyclopedia of Science and Technology, 7th ed. New York: McGraw-Hill 1992, 20 vols.

The New Palgrave: A Dictionary of Economics. New York: Stockton Press, 1998. 4 vols.

Almanacs, Yearbooks, Handbooks, Directories
Bartlett, John. *Familiar Quotations*, 16th ed. Boston: Little, Brown & Co., 1992.

Handbook of Chemistry and Physics. 1st Student ed., 1988. Boca Raton, Fla: Chemical Rubber Company Press, 1913- .

Information Please Almanac. Boston: Houghton Mifflin, 1974- .

Kane, Joseph N. *Famous First Facts*, 4th ed. New York: H. W. Wilson, 1997.

Statesman's Year-Book. New York: St. Martin's Press, 1864- .

World Almanac and Book of Facts. New York: World Almanac, 1868- .

Specialized Handbooks, Manuals
Consumer's Resource Handbook. Washington D.C.: United States Office of Consumer Affairs, 1992.

Masterplots : 1,801 plot stories and critical evaluations of the world's finest literature / edited by Frank N. Magill; story editor, revised edition, Dayton Kohler. Rev. 2nd ed. Pasadena, Calif.: Salem Pess, 1996. 12 vols. Expanded and updated version of the 1976 rev.ed.

Maps, Atlases, Gazetteers
Maps are produced by numerous governmental and private publishers (e.g., *the U.S. Geological Survey*, Central Intelligence Agency, AAA, National Geographic, Rand McNally, H. M. Gousha, General Drafting, Hammond).

Historical Atlas of the United States. Washington, D.C.: National Geographic Society, 1988. [thematic]

National Geographic Atlas of the World, 6th rev. ed. Washington, D.C.: National Geographic Society, 1992. [medium-size world]

Rand McNally *New Cosmopolitan World Atlas, census/environmental ed.* Chicago: Rand McNally, 1991. [medium-size]

Chambers World Gazetteer: *A Geographical Dictionary*. Cambridge: Cambridge University Press, 1990.

Biographical Sources
Contemporary Authors, 1981- . New revision series. Detroit: Gale Research.

U.S. General and Specialized Sources
American Men & Women of Science: A biographical dictionary of today's leaders in physical, biological and related sciences, 20th ed. New Providence, N. J. : R. R. Bowker, 1998. 8 vols.

Who's Who in America, 1899- . Chicago, Ill. : A. N. Marquis. Biennial.

World General Sources of Deceased Persons
Dictionary of Scientific Biography. New York: Scribner, 1970-1990, 8 vols., suppl.

Webster's New Biographical Dictionary. Springfield, Mass.: Merriam-Webster, 1988.

U.S. general and specialized sources of deceased persons
Biographical Directory of the American Congress, 1774-1996. Alexandria, Va.: CQ Staff Directories, Inc., 1997.

Dictionary of American Biography. New York: Scribner, 1973-1994.

Notable American Women, 1607-1950. A biographical dictionary.
Cambridge, Mass. : Belknap Press of Harvard University Press, 1971, 3
vols., suppls.

Searching For Reviews Online
<http://sunsite.berkeley.edu/Literature/>

<http://www.ala.org/booklist/index.html>

<http://www.nybooks.com/nyrev/index.html>

<http://www.latimes.com/>

<http://nytimes.com/>

ProQuest

NewsBank

Literary Criticism
Contemporary Literary Criticism. 2nd ed. New York: Longman, 1989.

*Masterplots : 2010 plot stories & essay reviews from the world's fine lit-
erature*, rev.ed. Frank N. Magill, ed. Englewood Cliffs, N.J.: Salem Press,
1976, 12 vols.

The Novel
American Novelists since World War II. Jeffrey Helterman and Richard
Layman, eds. Detroit: Gale Research, 1978.

Contemporary Novelists. James Vinson and D. L. Kirkpatrick, eds. 4th ed.
New York: St. Martin's, 1986.

Essay and General Literature Index. New York: Wilson, 1934- .
Semiannual.

Online magazine and newspaper databases
(also known as periodical indexes)
School libraries will probably use some of the online magazine and newspaper services, such as ***ProQuest*** or ***NewsBank*** to access newspaper,
magazine, and journal articles. Most of the indexes listed below will be

available in larger public and college libraries; we list some of these titles here because we want you to get familiar with some of these titles for future reference and perhaps use.

The Columbia Granger's Index to Poetry. 10th completely revised ed. Edited by Edith P. Hazen. New York: Columbia University Press, 1994.

General Science Index. Bronx, N.Y.: Wilson, 1978- . Monthly.

Humanities Index. Bronx, N.Y.: Wilson, 1974- . Monthly.

Play Index. Bronx, N.Y.: Wilson, 1952- . Irregular.

Readers' Guide to Periodical Literature. Bronx, N.Y.: Wilson, 1901-

Short Story Index. Bronx, Bronx, N.Y.: Wilson, 1953- . Annual

Song Index. Edited by Minnie Earl Sears. [n. p.] Shoe String Press, 1966.

About the Author

Dr. Ercegovac earned her Master's in Ethnomusicology (1973) and MLS (1975), both from the University of Illinois at Urbana-Champaign. She then moved to California and worked as a librarian and lecturer, and decided to go back to school for her doctorate (University of California, Los Angeles, 1990).

She has published widely in premier scholarly journals, including *Journal of the American Society for Information Science* (JASIS), *Information Processing and Management*, *Annual Review of the Information Science and Technology* (ARIST), *Cataloging & Classification Quarterly*, *College and Research Libraries*, *Library & Information Science Research*, *Reference Librarian*, and many others. She was a guest editor of the November issue (1999) of JASIS on metadata.

Dr. Ercegovac has contributed in the area of information literacy research. After she had taught hundreds of college students at UCLA for 8 years, she was convinced that information literacy does not start at the college level. It starts much earlier. Her classroom experience with college students, 7-12 students, and other populations, has convinced her that there is a commonality among information seeking behavior regardless of the searchers' age and individual differences. In 1995 Ercegovac founded an IL consulting firm, InfoEN Associates, that focuses on collaborative and problem-based learning, metacognition, and curriculum-embedded information literacy.

Her new book, *INFORMATION LITERACY: Search Strategies, Tools & Resources for High School Students*, published by Linworth Publishing in 2001, is the product of empirical research, classroom testing, collaboration with teachers, and yes, work with students. It is also based on readings in the areas of educational psychology, information seeking behavior of young adults, and information retrieval.

Dr. Ercegovac has been professionally active, contributing to the California School Library Association with workshops and presentations. She has contributed to the American Society for Information Science (ASIS) as a writer (2 papers in 1992; one paper in 1998), a guest editor (1999), and a reviewer. She is invited nationally (e.g., ASIS, IFLA in 2001) and internationally (COBISS Annual Conference in Maribor, Slovenia in 2000) as a speaker; she also participated at invited workshops (e.g., National Academy of Science in 1998; National Science Foundation workshop in 1998), and conferences. She is a review panelist at various funding agencies. For details, please see her Web page at: <http://www.cs.ucla.edu.Leap/zer/>.

Index